Creating the Curriculum

Is there an 'ideal' primary school curriculum?
Who should decide what the curriculum is?
Should teachers have autonomy over how they teach?

The curriculum is the heart of what teachers teach and learners learn: effective teaching is only possible with an effective curriculum. Yet in spite of its importance, there has been a crisis in curriculum that has been caused in large part by governments assuming direct control over the curriculum, assessment and, increasingly, pedagogy.

Creating the Curriculum tackles this thorny issue head on, challenging student and practising primary school teachers to think critically about past and present issues and to engage with a new wave of curriculum thinking and development. Considering curriculum construction and its impact on teaching and learning in the four countries of the UK, key issues considered include:

- who should decide the curriculum, its aims and its values;
- the extent to which issues in primary education swing back and forth;
- subjects versus thematic organisation, stages and phases, progression, breadth and balance;
- prescription versus teacher autonomy;
- the key features of effective classroom practice;
- strategies for assessing the whole curriculum;
- how language in the classroom influences curriculum design;
- understanding curricula in the context of children's social and personal circumstances;
- creativity, curriculum and the classroom.

Illustrated throughout with strategies and case studies from the classroom, *Creating the Curriculum* accessibly links the latest research and evidence with concrete examples of good practice. It is a timely exploration of what makes an effective and meaningful curriculum and how teachers can bring new relevance, motivation and powerful values to what they teach.

Dominic Wyse is Professor of Early Childhood and Primary Education at the Institute of Education, University of London, UK.

Vivienne Marie Baumfield is Professor of Pedagogy at the School of Education, University of Glasgow, UK.

David Egan is Emeritus Professor and Director at the Centre for Applied Education Research, Cardiff School of Education, University Wales in Cardiff, UK.

Carmel Gallagher is Research Associate at the School of Education, Queen's University, Belfast, UK.

Louise Hayward is Professor of Educational Assessment and Innovation at the School of Education, College of Social Sciences, University of Glasgow, UK.

Moira Hulme is Lecturer in Educational Research at the School of Education, University of Glasgow, UK.

Ruth Leitch is Professor of Education at the School of Education, Queen's University Belfast, UK.

Bob Lingard is Professorial Research Fellow at the School of Education, The University of Queensland, Australia.

Kay Livingston is Professor of Educational Research, Policy and Practice at the School of Education, University of Glasgow, UK.

Ian Menter is Professor of Teacher Education and Director of Professional Programmes at the Department of Education at the University of Oxford, UK.

The understanding primary education series

Edited by Dominic Wyse
The Institute of Education, University of London, UK

The understanding primary education series offers a fresh approach to key topics in primary education, combining compelling practical writing with rigorous theoretical and evidence-based argument. Breaking new ground in both established topics and essential topics which have been less well covered previously, the series emphasises the importance of research evidence, theory and reflection on practice in primary education. The series will be invaluable reading for all those engaged with initial teacher education and professional development who want authoritative accounts of issues central to working in the primary classroom.

Creating the Curriculum

Dominic Wyse,
Vivienne Marie Baumfield,
David Egan, Carmel Gallagher,
Louise Hayward, Moira Hulme,
Ruth Leitch, Kay Livingston
and Ian Menter, with Bob Lingard

Routledge
Taylor & Francis Group

LONDON AND NEW YORK

First published 2013
by Routledge
2 Park Square, Milton Park, Abingdon, Oxon OX14 4RN

Simultaneously published in the USA and Canada
by Routledge
711 Third Avenue, New York, NY 10017

Routledge is an imprint of the Taylor & Francis Group, an informa business

British Library Cataloguing in Publication Data
A catalogue record for this book is available from the British Library

Library of Congress Cataloging in Publication Data
Creating the curriculum/authored by Dominic Wyse . . . [et al.].
    p.cm – (Understanding primary education series)
  1. Curriculum planning–Great Britain. 2. Education, Elementary–Curricula–Great Britain. I. Wyse, Dominic, 1964– II. Title.
  LB2806.15.C69125 2012
  375'.001–dc23
                                                   2012008151

ISBN: 978–0–415–68769–0 (hbk)
ISBN: 978–0–415–68770–6 (pbk)
ISBN: 978–0–203–11591–6 (ebk)

Typeset in Galliard
by Swales & Willis Ltd, Exeter, Devon

Printed and bound in Great Britain by the MPG Books Group

Contents

Series editor's introduction

The curriculum is a vital feature of teaching and learning. The teacher's role requires them to plan the curriculum for their pupils in collaboration with other colleagues in the school. Teachers across the world are engaged in these processes. One significant variation for teachers internationally is the extent to which the nation state prescribes the curriculum that they must teach. In some countries teachers have great autonomy, in other countries they have less. The late twentieth century was characterised by many countries assuming greater state control over teachers and the curriculum. However, following disturbing evidence that greater state control was not necessarily a feature of the most effective curricula, doubts about such policies began to emerge. We now find ourselves in a period of uncertainty. Claims are made by some governments that greater control by teachers is necessary, although the reality of achieving this is being linked to less obvious forms of control over particular aspects of education, such as the necessity for schools to move from local authority control to academy or free school status if they are to benefit from enhanced funding and more freedom over the curriculum. But there are some genuine opportunities for greater autonomy over the curriculum, something that leads to questions about the kind of curricula that teachers and schools might create and implement.

In the early 1980s the primary classroom in the UK was described as a *secret garden* because of the autonomy that teachers and schools had over their practice. As a consequence of the enactment of the Education Reform Act 1988 the secret garden became a 'national park'. The law required that the Secretary of State for Education should create a national curriculum. Since that time debate has raged about the merits of a national curriculum, and about various aspects such as the amount of subject content, and the links with statutory assessment (SATs as they are commonly known). As a result of devolution the curricula of Northern Ireland, Scotland and Wales became increasingly different from that of England from the late 1990s onwards. The developments provide a fascinating opportunity for comparison. This book draws particularly on the experiences of England, Northern Ireland, Scotland and Wales in their development of curricula to see what lessons can be learned.

At the time of writing this book I had been working with the authors for several years as part of the CAPeR (Curriculum, Assessment, and Pedagogy Reform) group. One of the features of the team is their experience not only of research but also of direct involvement with government policy, and their experience as teacher educators and teachers. They bring their unique experience and knowledge to bear on how curricula might be created. A book like this also shows the rich potential for curriculum study, an area that some have argued has been in crisis, and one that is due for much greater focus now and in future.

Acknowledgements

We would particularly like to thank Helen Pritt, Suzanne Richardson and Rhiannon Findlay, and the many other Routledge staff, for their work with us on this book and on the series.

As series editor and author for this book Dominic would particular like to thank Bob Lingard for his introduction that became a powerful chapter in its own right, and to all the writers of this book with whom it continues to be such a genuine pleasure to work.

Bob Lingard would like to thank Dr Sam Sellar for his comments on drafts of his chapter.

This book is dedicated to teachers who create exciting curricula for their pupils, and passion for learning, in spite of the constraints that are a result of poor government policy.

Chapter 1

Reshaping the message systems of schooling in the UK

A critical reflection

Bob Lingard

> . . . differences within and change in the organization, transmission and evaluation of educational knowledge should be a major area of sociological interest.
>
> (Bernstein, 1971, p.47)

Introduction

The chapters in this collection deal with what Bernstein (1971) called the message systems of schooling – namely, curriculum, pedagogy and evaluation – that are now framed and function in an increasingly globalised and politicised education policy context. The chapters also focus on formalised statements of the aims of schooling in that context. The specific emphasis is the way the message systems and aims are changing in primary schools in England, Scotland, Wales and Northern Ireland, recently and also set against the *longue durée*.

As the Bernstein quote at the beginning of this reflection notes, changes in the message systems should be of interest to sociologists of education. That is the perspective I will take in this chapter. I would also note that the chapters are located outside of the sociology of education and outside of policy sociology of education, except for Chapter 6 on curriculum construction that utilises Gale's (2001) 'policy historiography' approach to its analysis. They fit more within curriculum studies and research dealing with pedagogy and assessment. In a Bourdieuian sense, curriculum studies as an area has been a distinct field of inquiry to policy sociology in education, which has dealt by and large with policies other than the message systems. My stance in this reflection is that these message systems are the central policy levers affecting the work of schools and teachers and as such a policy sociology perspective has something to offer in understanding the reshaping that is the focus of the collection. Furthermore, and as I will show below, Bernstein's evaluation mechanism has become associated with high stakes testing and a range of related account-abilities, which fit within a broader policy assemblage or ensemble. New accountabilities are central to the new policy assemblage and as such a policy sociology approach would seem to have real possibilities for understanding the reshaping of these message systems in the constituent schooling systems of the UK.

It is worth noting that as knowledge economy discourses have taken hold, and as the economy has been globalised, schooling policy has become more centralised and taken out of the hands of educators in what we might see as the 'economisation' of schooling policy (Rizvi and Lingard, 2010). Human capital production has become a more explicit and expressed purpose of schooling, even primary schooling, with economists and other non-educators framing meta-policy in education. This has implications for policy implementation by teachers in classrooms and also for the morale of the profession. Policy is developed away from teachers, but teachers are held fully accountable for student and school performance. As Coffield (2012) notes, politicians and policy-makers in education have been attracted to the McKinsey Reports (Barber and Mourshed, 2007; Mourshed *et al.*, 2010) as sources of policy reform, given their narrowed focus on quality teachers and quality school leaders, which overstates the research evidence on teacher and leader effects and denies very real contextual effects on the performance of both students and schools located in different socio-economic communities. Furthermore, we know inequality has been growing in the UK with implications for the work of schools and teachers and for the differences schools and teachers can make. This is not to say that schools cannot make a difference – they can, but within the constraints of their communities and the capitals of various kinds possessed or not by young people in those communities (Hayes *et al.*, 2006; Condron, 2011). The result of flawed mono-causal accounts of school effectiveness, particularly when accompanied by new performance-based accountabilities, is unconscionable pressure on teachers, leading to teaching by numbers (Taubman, 2009), lack of trust in teachers as professionals, and a disheartened profession. However, I would suggest that the current stress on quality teaching at least gives recognition to the importance of the profession, albeit decontextualised from social inequalities and unequal distribution of the capitals necessary for good school performance.

My stance is that we need more teacher involvement in policy production and more trust placed in teachers as professionals, with strong systemic commitment to and support for their ongoing professional development and proper salary structures. The questions for readers to think about and debate, interspersed throughout the chapters of this collection, are recognition of support by all authors for a stronger teacher/professional involvement in policy development and practice. As Andreas Schleicher (2008), Head of the Indicators and Analysis Division of the Education Directorate at the OECD, has noted, the best schooling systems involve a creative mix of 'informed prescription' at the policy producing centre and 'informed professionalism' at school and classroom sites. There are variations set against this ideal type in the cases of England, Wales, Scotland and Northern Ireland, with evidence of uninformed prescription in England and a lack of trust in teachers as non-educators have taken control of policy production and as new accountabilities have emerged. This lack of trust is endemic to the new managerialism, which functions across the public sector and which is accompanied by 'evidence-based' policy (Wiseman, 2010) and governing through numbers and data (Ozga, 2009; Lingard, 2011). Global pressures have seen a trend towards uninformed prescription in most schooling systems, as economic framings of schooling policy have strengthened and test-oriented accountability frameworks have dented levels of teacher professionalism.

In what follows, I initially seek to contextualise the reshaping of the message systems in both global and UK contexts, commenting as well on the imbrications of the political reshaping of schooling in the UK in relation to global contexts and pressures. The changing political structure of the UK can be seen to be mediating these pressures in the cases illustrated in this book: post-1999 devolution to Wales, Scotland and Northern Ireland is a good case in point. I then provide an indirect commentary on the contents of this collection through a focus on the three message systems. In my commentary, I seek to compare these in passing with developments elsewhere and globally. This commentary aims to illustrate the interweaving of the global, national and historical in contemporary developments in primary schooling.

Contexts of the message systems

Bernstein's three message systems sit in a symbiotic relationship with each other, with changes in one system being reflected in changes in the other. They are also central to the cultural and social reproduction roles of schooling: that is, the role of knowledge in reproducing dominant cultural patterns and in the reproduction of inequality from generation to generation. Bernstein (2004, p.205) has argued that success at school in social class terms requires a home pedagogy complementary to that of school; a reality more common for middle-class children. This is a similar analysis to Bourdieu's account of the capitals that are necessary for ease of relationships with schooling and for outstanding academic performance. These capitals are central to the way that he sees schools, through their use of concepts such as ability, as misrecognising the social gift of cultural capital as an individual intellectual trait. In later work, Bernstein (2004) spoke of pedagogy as a 'cultural relay' in referring to these exogenous purposes and connections of schooling.

These theoretical observations are evident in the narratives about changes to the message systems and in the aims of schooling included in this collection. Today, however, we need to recognise the strength of globalised education policy discourses and their effects, including from supranational political entities such as the European Union (EU), despite subsidiarity, and from international organisations such as the OECD. These discourses and effects are played out in vernacular ways within specific societies and particular systems of schooling. Further, there are clear differences across the constituent parts of the UK in respect of the EU and schooling. Scotland, for example, draws on EU membership and works with other European nations as a way of fostering its own national aspirations to differentiate itself from England, which seems more indifferent to the EU. These particular relationships with supra- and international policy processes and organisations intersect with idiosyncratic national contexts and histories. For example, the more social democratic aspects of contemporary schooling policy in Scotland also probably reflect the long Scottish Enlightenment tradition in schooling stretching back to the eighteenth century (Lingard, 2008).

Global pressures are evident in the UK, but they have been mediated in varying ways (Ball, 2008, p.2) by the reworking of UK politics and policy-making following the Blair government's strategy of 'political devolution' and granting of greater decision-making power in respect of schools in 1999 to the 'governments'/'assemblies' of Scotland, Wales and Northern Ireland. This complexifying of UK policy-making and politics in schooling is both a response to and an expression of new forms of nationalism in the context of global pressures towards cultural homogenisation. As Appadurai (2006) argues, 'ethnos' and national identities are things nations seek to hold onto in the globalised context of weakened national sovereignty in economic and political matters, and schooling plays a role in this atavism. The lack of support for the language resources available in the diverse multicultural UK is interesting in this respect, as is support for bilingualism in the Welsh and Northern Ireland curricula, and some support for Gaelic in Scotland. It is also noteworthy that as English has become the language of the global economy, and the numbers of people learning English around the globe have exploded, that the teaching of foreign languages in English-speaking countries is in sharp decline. These localised differences are demonstrated across the chapters, for example, in the varying expressions of the aims of schooling in Northern Ireland and in Scotland.

My argument here is that there has been a tendency for the evaluation message system to be reduced to testing (often high stakes) and tightly linked to accountability regimes. Furthermore, *such testing has taken the upper hand as the major steering message system of schooling*, at least in Western advanced nations in thrall to neo-liberal policy verities. As Stobart (2008, p.24) has put it:

> A key purpose of assessment, particularly in education, has been to establish and raise standards of learning. This is now a virtually universal belief – it is hard to find a country that is not using the rhetoric of needing assessment to raise standards in response to the challenges of globalization.

Nonetheless such pressures are played out in the systems we are focusing on here in very specific ways. Thus Wales and Scotland have much less standardised testing than has been the case in England.

Additionally, as I have argued elsewhere (Lingard and Rawolle, 2011; Lingard, 2011), we have also seen in the context of globalisation an emergent global education policy field. This field is being constituted through the increasing policy salience of national comparative school system performance data such as the OECD's Programme for International Student Assessment (PISA) and the International Association for the Evaluation of Educational Achievement's (IEA) Trends in Maths and Science Study (TIMSS) and Progress in International Reading Literacy Study (PIRLS). Related, we see the rise of a global epistemic community, which helps constitute the global field, as do globalised education policy discourses. These tests and other related global data on schooling systems (e.g. the OECD's *Education at a Glance* reports and the development of global educational indicators conjointly by the OECD, UNESCO and the World Bank) constitute the globe as a commensurate space of measurement of the comparative performance of national schooling systems. This is an example, as Novoa and Yariv-Mashal (2003, p.427) suggest, of 'the politics of mutual accountability' and global and national governance working through the coming together of the 'global eye' and the 'national eye': what can be seen as 'governing through data' and comparison (Ozga, 2009, p.159). In this respect, Torrance (1997) speaks of a 'globalising empiricism' driving contemporary education policy.

International comparative data have been a factor in policy convergence across very different national schooling systems, encouraging national testing and some broader policy alignments. For example, Korea has set national targets for improvement on PISA, while Brazil has restructured much of its curriculum around the application of knowledge central to PISA tests. Malaysia has decided to participate in PISA in 2012 as part of their strategy of international benchmarking to be used to enhance school performance towards the goal of achieving developed nation status by 2020. We also see changes in 'reference societies' in terms of policy borrowing and policy learning: Finland became the PISA 'poster boy', while China's, or rather Shanghai's, performance on the 2009 PISA has been used by President Obama in the United States to call for a renewed focus on quality schooling. It is interesting in this respect that for the OECD the UK is the unit of analysis. However, the constituent parts of the UK now fund the disaggregation of OECD PISA data for their devolved governments. It is also interesting how the Coalition government in the UK has made more rhetorical usage of PISA data, as ammunition for its desired education policy changes in England, than did the previous Blair/Brown New Labour governments, which held great faith in national school performance data. It appears that PISA data are also currently being used in this way in Wales. Regarding international comparative data on schooling performance, Wiseman (2010, p.18) notes,

> what widely available international data on education has done is create an intellectual space where educational policymaking is not geographically or politically bounded but is instead bounded by the extent of the legitimated evidence used to support one decision or policy versus another.

This forms part of the globalised phenomenon of 'evidence-based' policy, but also aligns with my argument that Bernstein's evaluation message system is being reduced to testing, which has become the major steering mechanism within many national schooling systems.

The chapters in this collection provide accounts of the salience of national performance data set against international comparisons and the related importance of the testing message system. Again, however, as the chapters show, this works differently in each of the systems, so that in Scotland there has been a concerted policy move towards assessment as, of and for learning, utilising the work of Paul Black and Dylan Wiliam, and less emphasis on high stakes testing and policy focused on improving test scores, as is the case in England. There have also been attempts in Scotland to align assessment practices with the new *Curriculum for Excellence*. And we also need to recognise that national systems use PISA data for political purposes, well beyond those suggested by their creators and analysts.

As the chapters demonstrably illustrate, these global and national 'policy as numbers' pressures are always played out in vernacular ways, set against specific histories, cultures and politics. As argued elsewhere in respect of policy developments, so too in respect of curricula change and other changes to the message system: 'There is always a prior history of significant events, a particular ideological climate, a social and economic context' (Taylor *et al.*, 1997, p.16).

In terms of endogenous UK policy pressures, what we see is increasing convergence flowing from the time of Thatcher's Education Reform Act of 1988, which created the first 'national curriculum' in England, and then enhanced divergence following the commitment to political devolution by the Blair government in 1999. There is a rider on this account of the 1988 Education Reform Act: Scotland continued to work outside of it with curriculum at the time still the responsibility of Local Authorities within Scotland. Both these patterns of convergence and divergence, however, were set against convergence pressures upon national systems emerging from the pressures of and responses to globalisation, both at EU level – less significant for England, more significant for the other systems – and international comparative performance data, as illustrated in the chapters in the collection.

Curriculum and aims of schooling

The focus of the chapters in this book is on primary schools in the constituent parts of the UK. In Chapter 2, Ian Menter talks about the three competing traditions of primary schooling that have emerged since the introduction of mass schooling in the nineteenth century (earlier in Scotland). These primary philosophies include traditions based on the three Rs and basic skills (the elementary tradition), those framed by knowledge structured around disciplines and Western high culture (the preparatory tradition), and those focused more on the child and developmental stages (the developmental tradition), beginning with Rousseau and moving through to Dewey and subsequent developmentalists (Piaget etc.). As Menter notes, there was also a class base to these different approaches. These traditions or philosophies of education have competed historically and are still evident in the different approaches to national primary curriculum in the systems examined here. It also should be noted that primary teachers probably hold quite strongly to a more progressive child-centred, developmental approach as argued for by Dewey in his US writings early in the twentieth century and by the 1967 Plowden Report in England. More recent curriculum developments, in England for example, have caused real consternation for teachers, as the curriculum has become more tightly framed, more fulsomely elaborated and more test-oriented, with strong challenges to child-centredness.

The chapters here speak of the curriculum now being 'delivered', rather than being utilised (especially in England) and put into practice by well-informed professional teachers who rework the formal curriculum by taking account of their students, their school and their community. The enacted curriculum is now more controlled by the formally articulated curriculum as education has become a central policy plank in broader economic and social policies in the UK. This is also the case in Australia, with the new national curriculum for English, maths, science and history from the preparatory primary year to year 10. As already noted, this 'national control' is linked to the 'economisation of education policy', including schooling policy, and the dominance of a human capital approach to policy (Rizvi and Lingard, 2010).

We should note, however, that elementary schooling from the outset also had other purposes, including citizenship goals. In many ways national primary schooling was about, in Benedict Anderson's (1991) terms, helping to constitute through mass literacy the 'imagined community' which was the nation. Further, in its earliest instantiation, primary schooling served different purposes for those from different social class backgrounds: elementary skills as preparation for work and access to discipline knowledge and high culture as preparation for more education and later university and the professions. This distinction has been blurred somewhat with participation of most young people in secondary schooling and a goal of 50 per cent of the age cohort attending university.

What we have seen is an upward credential spiral. Political devolution can also be seen, at least in Scotland and Wales, as a way of strengthening the purposes of primary schooling in respect of identities, helping to strengthen the imagined communities of Scotland and Wales within the UK and globally.

We also need to note the 'selective tradition' of the curriculum, to draw on Raymond Williams' concept which has been utilised most productively by Michael Apple in his 1979 classic text within curriculum studies: *Ideology and the Curriculum*. From all that could be taught, selective decisions are taken about what to include at what stages and for whom. Debates about the current content of the history curriculum in England (and in Australia, where history is one of the four initial school subjects of the new P-10 national curriculum) are manifestations of this selective tradition.

It could be argued that in England, testing regimes and the national curriculum set the de facto aims of schooling. This is the case despite the articulation in 2000 by the Qualifications and Curriculum Authority of an elaborate statement of the aims of schooling for England, which were very broad and concerned with the development of the whole child ('spiritual, moral, social and cultural development'). However, as Carmel Gallagher and Dominic Wyse argue in Chapter 3, this statement remained disjunctive with the effects of testing and self-referential national curricula. The same is the case in Australia where there are two broad goals for all schools, agreed to by all governments and schooling systems. These are: 'Goal 1: Australian schooling promotes equity and excellence. Goal 2: All young Australians become: successful learners, confident and creative individuals, active and informed citizens' (Ministerial Council on Education, Employment, Training and Youth Affairs, 2008, p.X). I would argue that national testing through the National Assessment Program – Literacy and Numeracy (NAPLAN), which works through tests for all students in all schools at years 3, 5, 7 and 9, has also dented the likelihood of all schools pursuing the broader articulated goals in Australia.

The aims of schooling in Wales are also interesting in their talk of Wales as *The Learning Nation* and the positioning of the aims against the UN's Convention on the Rights of the Child. Related, I would note the way in which education policy in the EU has become rearticulated as 'learning policy'. As Gallagher and Wyse note in Chapter 3, this reference to the UN Convention raises questions about the extent to which the rights of the child should be at the centre of schooling, including curricula. The objectives of schooling in Northern Ireland focus on goals for individuals, the production of 'Contributors' 'to Society' and 'to the Economy and Environment'. In Scotland the Curriculum for Excellence has four capacities as its curricular aims: 'successful learners', 'confident individuals', 'responsible citizens' and 'effective contributors'. The important point about the Scottish situation is the alignment with curriculum, the attempt to align with assessment practices, and also the fact that the Curriculum for Excellence applies across the 3–19 years age groups. Effective schooling systems defined in relation to these broader purposes of schooling would work towards alignment across curriculum, pedagogy and assessment and with the goals of schooling. Louise Hayward makes this point very well in Chapter 5 on assessment in the primary school, with her stress on assessment being a central component of curriculum planning at school and class-room levels and emphasis on the intimate coexistence of pedagogy and assessment for learning.

Pedagogy

As noted in several chapters, pedagogy is not a word used regularly or indeed easily in the UK by teachers. It is more common in Europe and framed there as broader than teaching to include structuring philosophies of education and the overarching purposes of schooling. As noted in Chapter 4, talk of pedagogy *à la* Dewey cuts across the knowledge to be taught and the characteristics of the child. Traditionally, pedagogy has not been articulated into public policy, rather it was something within the professional purview of the classroom teacher and structured to some extent by curricula and assessment practices. Further, as Alexander's (2000, p.5) monumental study of pedagogy across five nations demonstrates, pedagogy is framed by different national traditions and cultures, 'ideas and values, habits and customs, institutions and world views'.

Interestingly, as the research evidence has strengthened regarding the great significance of teachers and their pedagogies (also inclusive of formative assessment practices in some definitions) for the enhancement of student learning (Hayes *et al.*, 2006; Hattie, 2009), policy in some systems has sought to frame pedagogy either directly, as in the New South Wales schooling system in Australia where there is a Quality Teaching policy that articulates the traits of high quality pedagogy, or implicitly as in England under New Labour through the National Literacy and Numeracy Strategies. There are dangers here, of course, such as technicising teachers' work and contributing to their deprofessionalisation. And while teachers and their practices are the central school-based factors in good student learning, contextual factors such as socio-economic inequalities are also very important. Condron (2011), in a recent article analysing PISA performance in the United States, actually argues the way to improvement for US PISA performance would be through confronting deep social inequalities and poverty and addressing the savage inequalities evidenced in the differential funding of schools located in different tax districts. Indeed, we often see in rich countries that students with the greatest advantages in life in terms of parental material well-being, and possession of other capitals necessary for success at school as demonstrated by Bourdieu, also have the most expended on their schooling. There is thus a real danger in the narrow focus on quality teachers and quality school leaders as the way to better school and systemic performance, as suggested by the two McKinsey Reports, particularly for schools in poor communities (Coffield, 2012).

It is interesting to note, in this context, how successful John Hattie's book (2009) *Visible Learning* has been in sales terms, as his meta-analysis is misread by policy-makers and schools to indicate that teachers alone make all the difference. Hattie rightly argues that he is only dealing with those practices schools and teachers can have effects on. He also acknowledges that other external factors, such as socio-economic circumstances and the like, might very well have more effect. Thus, he states,

> It is not a book about what cannot be influenced in schools – thus critical discussions about class, poverty, resources in families, and nutrition are not included – but this is NOT because they are unimportant, indeed they may be more important than many of the influences discussed in this book.

(pp. viii–ix)

Having said that, he does stress the great significance of 'reducing the variability in the impact of teachers (or more importantly raising the impact of all)' (Hattie, 2011, p.9), a position with which I agree. In this respect, though, I would say that the high stakes testing approach attached to accountability reduces the emphasis on intellectual demand in pedagogies and thus potentially reduces the impact of the teacher.

The last point I want to make about pedagogy is the way that high stakes testing can reshape pedagogy, one message system affecting another. This situation is reflected in talk of 'teaching to the test' and 'teaching by numbers'. I would suggest that in terms of schooling and social justice, that test-driven systems such as that in England have greatest impact on those schools not doing well on the tests, often those serving poor communities. There is a way in which the resulting pedagogies in such schools reinforce curriculum inequalities between schools located in different social class contexts, with teaching to the test in schools in poor communities reproducing societal inequalities in the way Jean Anyon (1981) described in her classic research study on social classes, curriculum and differentiated pedagogies. In a reprise of Anyon's classic study, Allan Luke (2010) provides a stinging critique of the 'scripted pedagogies' that result from teaching to the test, and observes, 'The key policies of scripted, standardized pedagogy risk offering working-class, cultural and linguistic minority students precisely what Anyon presciently described: an enacted curriculum of basic skills, rule recognition and compliance' (p.180). What was the focus of Anyon's critique has been instantiated in some schools as the effect of high stakes testing. In Hattie's terms, this situation will minimise the educative impact of teachers, rather than maximise it and this will be particularly the case in schools serving poor communities.

Evaluation and testing

I have noted in some detail the significance of such testing to the reframing of enacted curriculum and pedagogy. I have argued that testing, central now to Bernstein's evaluation message system, has become a significant steering mechanism of schooling and that there are both global and national aspects to this. Stephen Ball (2008) has argued that there are three policy technologies driving contemporary schooling systems framed by neo-liberalism, namely, the new managerialism, performativity and markets and choice discourses. Testing and related data flows are linked to each of these policy technologies. The system steers at a distance through data, the system is kept commensurate through data, and markets and choice to some extent also work through comparative performance data. Lyotard's (1984) interesting work on the function of performativity, in a post-Cold War world where meta-narratives are in decline, suggests that systemic sustainability functions through it: systems must be 'be operational (that is commensurable) or disappear' (p.xxiv). Ball (2006, 2008) develops this concept and applies it productively to contemporary neo-liberal education policy regimes, noting:

> Performativity is a technology, a culture and a mode of regulation that employs judgments, comparisons and displays as a means of incentive, control, attrition and change – based on rewards and sanctions (both material and symbolic). The per-

formances (of individual subjects or organisations) serve as a measure of productivity or output or displays of 'quality'.

(Ball, 2006, p.144)

Here we see comparison as a mode of governance, a mode clearly evident in the global and national uses of PISA and national uses of other performance data. There are the related issues, Ball observes, of who now controls the field of judgment: the policy-makers, the test constructors, the statisticians, the technical fraction of the middle class with such expertise who work now within a global epistemic community. We see here another challenge to teacher professionalism. Ball again:

> The issue of who controls the field of judgment is crucial. One key issue of the current educational reform movement may be seen as struggles over the control of the field of judgment and its values.

(Ball, 2006, p.144)

I fully concur that one central debate within contemporary schooling policy around the globe, and in the England, Scotland, Wales and Northern Ireland, is the question of who controls the field of judgment and contests over the values that are deeply embedded within it.

Concluding comments

What I have argued in this reflection is that globalisation has provoked an emergent transnational education policy field, which creates a global system of mutual account-ability in respect of national schooling, where it has had real effects. In national systems of schooling, testing regimes, linked to accountability framed around test performance, complement these transnational developments. The chapters in this collection well illustrate this new form of policy steering with effects within and across the message systems, as testing dominates the evaluation message system with consequences for both curricula and pedagogy and also for teachers' work. Additionally, the chapters also demonstrate, describe and deconstruct vernacular expressions and effects of these global pressures and national recontextualising of them. They also illustrate the ways in which the Blair policy of devolving more decision-making powers in schooling to Scotland, Wales and Northern Ireland was a response to, and expression of, both globalisation and new nationalisms. The message systems and schooling policy in England are perhaps the clearest articulation of the argument proffered here. Differences in the message systems in Scotland, Northern Ireland and Wales reflect specific histories, politics and local struggles that have mediated global and UK education policy discourses. One has to wonder what the impact of ongoing global economic crises, instabilities and a politics of austerity will be on the message systems of schooling and indeed on these policy regimes and their varying responses to global, national and local political pressures.

References

Alexander, R. (2000) *Culture and Pedagogy: International Comparisons in Primary Education*, London, Blackwell.

Anderson, B. (1991) (revised edition) *Imagined Communities*, London, Verso.

Anyon, J. (1981) Social class and school knowledge, *Curriculum Inquiry*, 15, pp.207–214.

Appadurai, A. (2006) *Fear of Small Numbers*, Durham, NC, Duke University Press.

Apple, M. (1979) *Ideology and Curriculum*, New York, Routledge.

Ball, S. (2006) *Education Policy and Social Class*, London, Routledge.

Ball, S. (2008) *The Education Debate*, Bristol, Policy Press.

Barber, M. and Mourshed, M. (2007) *How the World's Best-Performing School Systems Come out on Top*, McKinsey & Company.

Bernstein, B. (1971) On the classification and framing of educational knowledge, in M.F.D. Young (ed.) *Knowledge and Control*, London, Collier-Macmillan, pp.47–69.

Bernstein, B. (2004) Social class and pedagogic practice, in S. Ball (ed.) *The RoutledgeFalmer Reader in Sociology of Education*, London, Routledge, pp.196–217.

Coffield, F. (2012) Why the McKinsey reports will not improve school systems, *Journal of Education Policy*, 27, 1, pp.131–149.

Condron, D. (2011) Egalitarianism and educational excellence, *Educational Researcher*, 40, 2, pp.47–55.

Gale, T. (2001) Critical policy sociology: historiography, archaeology and genealogy as methods of policy analysis, *Journal of Education Policy*, 16, 5, pp.379–393.

Hattie, J. (2009) *Visible Learning: A Synthesis of Over 800 Meta-Analyses Relating to Achievement*, London, Routledge.

Hattie, J. (2011) Purposes and uses of educational research, *Professional Magazine* (Queensland Teachers' Union), 26, pp.8–10.

Hayes, D., Mills, M., Christie, P. and Lingard, B. (2006) *Schools and Teachers Making a Difference*, Sydney, Allen & Unwin.

Lingard, B. (2008) Scottish Education: reflections form an international perspective, in T.G.K. Bryce and W.M. Humes (eds) (3rd edition) *Scottish Education Beyond Devolution*, Edinburgh, University of Edinburgh Press, pp.968–981.

Lingard, B. (2011) Policy as numbers: ac/counting, *The Australian Educational Researcher*, 37, 1, pp.355–382.

Lingard, B. and Rawolle, S. (2011) New scalar politics: implications for education policy, *Comparative Education*, 47, 4, pp.489–502.

Luke, A. (2010) Documenting reproduction and inequality: revisiting Jean Anyon's 'Social class and school knowledge', *Curriculum Inquiry*, 40, pp.167–182.

Lyotard, J.-F. (1984) *The Postmodern Condition*, Manchester, Manchester University Press.

Ministerial Council on Education, Employment, Training and Youth Affairs (2008) *Melbourne Declaration on Educational Goals for Young Australians*, Canberra, MCEETYA.

Mourshed, M., Chijioke, C. and Barber, M. (2010) *How the World's Most Improved School Systems Keep Getting Better*. McKinsey & Company.

Novoa, A. and Yariv-Mashal, Y. (2003) Comparative research in education: a mode of governance or a historical journey?, *Comparative Education*, 39, 4, pp.423–438.

Ozga, J. (2009) Governing education through data in England: from regulation to self-evaluation, *Journal of Education Policy*, 24, 2, pp.149–162.

Rizvi, F. and Lingard, B. (2010) *Globalizing Education Policy*, London, Routledge.

Schleicher, A. (2008) Seeing school systems through the prism of PISA, in A. Luke, K. Weir and A. Woods (eds) *Development of a Set of Principles to Guide a P-12 Syllabus Framework*, Brisbane, Queensland Studies Authority, pp.72–85.

Stobart, G. (2008) *Testing Times: The Uses and Abuses of Assessment*, London, Routledge.

Taubman, P. (2009) *Teaching by Numbers*, New York, Routledge.

Taylor, S., Rizvi, F., Lingard, B. and Henry, M. (1997) *Educational Policy and the Politics of Change*, London, Routledge.

Torrance, H. (1997) Assessment, accountability, and standards: using assessment to control the reform of schooling, in A.H. Halsey, H. Lauder, P. Brown and A. Stuart Well (eds) *Education Culture Economy Society*, Oxford, Oxford University Press, pp.320–331.

Wiseman, A. (2010) The uses of evidence for educational policy-making: global contexts and international trends, in A. Luke, J. Green and G. Kelly (eds) *What Counts as Evidence and Equity? Review of Research in Education*, New York, AERA, pp.1–24.

Chapter 2

The history of primary education and the curriculum

Ian Menter

Chapter summary

This chapter examines the history and nature of primary education in the UK, including its boundaries and links with early years and secondary education. A number of competing traditions have been seen to influence the shaping of the primary school curriculum. What emerges is a complex picture with some variation between the four nations of the UK and a number of significant political interventions, especially towards the end of the twentieth century. The role and responsibilities of teachers in relation to the school curriculum have been a matter of considerable change and we begin to see how the professional identities of primary school teachers relate as much to children as they do to knowledge.

Introduction

It was during the 1950s that primary education became firmly established as a distinctive phase of compulsory education in the UK. In this chapter we trace these developments from their origins until the present and see how the curriculum of the primary school has been shaped and changed in response to this trajectory.

The primary school is very much a British conception. It emerged during the twentieth century in slightly different ways in each part of Britain and draws on a range of influences, as we shall see. We examine three key periods in the development of primary schooling. First, the period up to 1967, the date at which the seminal report by the Plowden Committee was published and only two years after the Primary Memorandum was published in Scotland. The second period runs from then until 1988 when the Education Reform Act set out new arrangements for the whole of the school curriculum. Third, we examine what has happened from 1988 until the present time. In the final section of the chapter we examine the role of teachers in making decisions about the curriculum that they teach, a theme that is picked up and examined in more detail in Chapter 4.

The making of the primary school in the twentieth century (up to 1967)

In his two-volume history of primary education, Alan Blyth identifies the three main traditions from which it draws (Blyth, 1965) the elementary, the preparatory and the developmental (or 'progressive').

The elementary tradition came from the emergence of universal educational provision in the nineteenth century. Elementary schools then were established by the churches and voluntary bodies. These schools concentrated on what later became known as 'the basics' or 'the three Rs', wRiting, Reading and aRithmetic. But these were taught within a strong framework of a fourth R, Religion, because in addition to ensuring literacy and numeracy, the schools were to provide a clear moral code, based on Christianity, through which children would learn to live harmoniously in society. In the early part of the twentieth century national requirements set out a wider framework of subjects including handiwork and nature study, much of which were taught through 'object lessons'.

The preparatory tradition on the other hand had its roots in private schooling established mainly to provide for the children of the more wealthy members of society – because they had to pay for this education – and was designed literally as preparation for later schooling which in turn would lead towards university. Such schooling also included the basics, where required, but with a greater emphasis on the full range of humanities and sciences, providing a route towards engagement with western European 'high' culture.

The developmental tradition was based around early theories of learning that focus on the child and saw education at an early age as needing to facilitate the interaction between the individual and his/her environment. The tradition drew on the ideas of philosophers such as Jean-Jacques Rousseau, who believed that the child would flourish if provided with the appropriate educative setting. This view lay behind the initiatives of educators such as Friedrich Froebel and Maria Montessori in Europe, and such as Margaret McMillan and Susan Isaacs in England. This tradition was most closely associated with the education of very young children but increasingly had some influence on the education of children throughout their first 11 years.

So we see three key themes emerging which would be in constant tension as primary schooling developed – 'basic skills', 'subjects' (and knowledge) and 'the child', each theme relating to one of the traditions. But we also begin to see that it is not possible entirely to separate the primary curriculum from questions of teaching and learning ('pedagogy'), nor indeed from the ways in which children and their learning are assessed.

Paradoxically, it was the Hadow Committee's 1926 report on *The Education of the Adolescent* that was the first formal declaration of primary education as a distinctive phase of schooling up to the age of 11. It was only gradually thereafter that elementary schools became divided into primary and secondary schools. The elementary tradition therefore formed the foundation of the primary school. However, as Galton *et al.* (1980) note, by the time of the first official report on the primary school in 1931 (the second Hadow Report), there was already some evidence of the developmental tradition having influence on provision for younger children. Indeed they argue that it was this 1931 report that offered the basis for 'a completely new approach to primary education' (p.35). They quote from the report thus: 'the curriculum of the primary school is to be thought of in terms of activity and experience, rather than of knowledge to be acquired and facts to be stored'. The report suggested that lessons might be taught through topics rather than traditional subjects.

As state schooling developed during the twentieth century so that eventually there was provision for all children to the ages of 15 and then 16, the primary and secondary stages became detached from each other. In a more general sense then primary education came to be seen as the preparation for secondary schooling. Secondary schooling was seen as having responsibility for preparing children to enter the workforce. So, one of the main functions of primary schooling was to induct young people into patterns of behaviour that are conducive to their own learning and to the successful preparation of pupils to function in the much larger educational institutions to which they would transfer. Indeed at certain times this preparation in the primary school has extended to a system of selection and differentiation at the end of primary schooling, with the purpose of identifying which pupils should go to which type of secondary school. This was most notable in the era following the Second World War where secondary schooling in some parts of the UK was arranged into 'tripartite' parallel streams of technical, secondary modern and grammar schools. Tests taken by children at the end of primary school were used as a major means of deciding which children would go to which type of school.

The boundaries of primary education only came to be established gradually, now usually being recognised as education for children between the ages of 4 or 5 and 11 or 12. The age for the commencement of compulsory schooling became the key factor in determining the starting age and transfer to secondary school became the equivalent for determining the concluding age. However there have been many debates about the appropriateness of particular starting and finishing points and indeed the idea of the middle school completely contradicts the common concept of primary education, being based on the notion that there should be three stages to compulsory schooling – first, middle and high – with the middle school typically covering the 8–13 age range.

Even within the 4/5–11 current conventional view of primary education, there are different internal forms of organisation. In many parts of Britain the primary range actually incorporates two distinctive substages, the infant (4/5–7) and the junior (7–11). The infant tradition emerged in large part from concern about the distinctive needs of younger children, as represented in part by the developmental tradition. Junior school was then the site of more formal learning of skills and subjects. As we shall see later, in England this conception was partly reinforced by the 1988 National Curriculum which divided primary education into two key stages (1 and 2) very much in line with the old infant/junior division. There was further ambiguity in the subsequent development of the 'Foundation Stage' covering the ages 3–5 ('early years' and 'reception') with a distinctive curriculum (see below).

Primary schools have developed as comprehensive institutions, that is they are set up to be available to (almost) all children. Other than the division between private and public provision (and more than 130,000 children in the 5–11 age range attend private schools in the UK) there is no formal differentiation between types of school in the way that there has been for secondary provision in some parts of the UK. This does not mean that there are not considerable tensions about who can attend which school. In densely populated urban areas there can be fierce competition to secure a place at a particularly popular school and so regulations and systems have had to be devised to regulate entry. At earlier times there was separate provision for boys and girls but that has been ended in the state sector for about 50 years. (Some schools in Northern Ireland, however, remain divided on gender lines.)

Not all state schools have the same form of governance however. Throughout the UK a significant proportion of primary schools are managed by one of the churches. For example, in England, about 25 per cent of schools are associated with the Church of England and about 10 per cent are Roman Catholic. In Scotland 15 per cent of primary schools are Roman Catholic. In Northern Ireland the percentage is much higher. The influence of the respective churches over the schools' curricula can be quite significant and certainly the churches often claim that their schools have a distinctive ethos (sometimes seen as indicative of the schools' 'hidden' curriculum).

As intimated above, the primary school and its curriculum were fully established during the 1950s. That is when the three traditions were first brought together and developed in a distinctive manner, effectively as part of what has been called the social democratic settlement that ensued from the Second World War. It was also around that period that teacher training started to develop in a more sustained way that involved an increasing amount of academic study. Primary teachers were still seen in some ways as subordinate in status to secondary teachers, but increasingly they moved towards professional parity.

To conclude our consideration of this period we can look at a handbook for primary teachers first published by the Ministry of Education in 1958 and recommended as part of their training over the following years (Ministry of Education, 1958). It was written by Her Majesty's Inspectors. The early sections of the book follow the structure of schooling from nursery through infant and then junior phases, discussing teaching methods and organisation, with clear evidence of a commitment to a developmental view of learning, but also to the need for discipline. The later section of the book is entitled 'Fields of Learning' and discusses the curriculum under the following headings:

- religion;
- physical education;
- language;
- mathematics;
- art and craft and needlework;
- handwriting;
- music;
- history;
- geography and natural history.

We shall see how much and how little has changed as we move through the next two periods.

Key questions for reflection

'In an ideal world', at what age do you think children should enter primary school and why?

'In an ideal world', at what age should children leave primary education and move into post-primary?

Tensions in the primary curriculum 1967–1987

During the 1960s there was increasing concern about social deprivation especially in inner urban areas and there were also emerging concerns about the increasing linguistic and ethnic diversity embodied in many urban primary school populations. These were among the issues that led to the establishment of the Plowden Committee which was set up by the government's advisory council and reported in 1967. This was a very wide ranging review, entitled *Children and their Primary Schools*, with the opening sentence: 'At the heart of the primary school lies the child.'

This appeared to foreground the developmental tradition and this influence was indeed very apparent in parts of the report. However there was still also plenty of interest in subjects and in basic skills. In retrospect, people have often referred to the 'Plowden ideology' of primary education, usually implying that this was heavily child-centred and over-emphasising the 'progressive' developmental tradition. An actual reading of the report belies this claim.

Much original research was carried out for this report including significant work that associated school achievement with family background. The report has much to say about literacy and numeracy, as well as about the key social role of the primary school within communities. Following the publication of the report, 'Educational Priority Areas' were established in many cities, where extra resources were allocated to support extra staffing and other forms of support in those areas that were seen to be most disadvantaged. The report also led to the development of support for learners of English as a Second Language (ESL) and saw the emergence of early approaches to 'multi-cultural education'.

But perhaps the most significant outcome of the report was the confirmation in the public mind that primary education was an important and distinctive element in educational policy and provision. In relation to the curriculum there is a clear emphasis on English and significant discussion of religious education. Mathematics does not get the high priority it was later to receive (nor does science). The notions of the 'integrated day' and the topic-based curriculum are discussed, but the most important principle in provision is that it should be flexible.

> Any practice which predetermines the pattern and imposes it upon all is to be condemned.

(para. 538)

There is little place for the type of scheme which sets down exactly what ground should be covered and what skill should be acquired by each class in the school.

(para. 539)

A commitment to curriculum flexibility and local determination had been rising to prominence during the 1960s largely through exciting and innovative work by individual teachers or groups of teachers and inspectors. Teachers such as Sybil Marshall and inspectors such as Christian Schiller and John Blackie were promoting integrated approaches to learning that focused very much on the child, indeed they were 'child-centred' (see Simon, 1991, ch.7).

In the Plowden Report, as in the texts that these leading practitioners were producing, there is discussion of 'discovery methods', the importance of 'free play', the 'integrated day' and 'learning through experience'.

One of the most important responsibilities of teachers is to help children to see order and pattern in experience, and to extend their ideas by analogies and by the provision of suitable vocabulary. Rigid division of the curriculum into subjects tends to interrupt children's trains of thought and of interest and to hinder them from realising the common elements in problem solving. These are among the many reasons why some work, at least, should cut across subject divisions at all stages in the primary school.

(Plowden, 1967, para. 535)

Although such imaginative and wholehearted approaches to primary teaching were relatively rare in practice, nevertheless there were some schools that were increasingly radical in their child-centredness. The late 1960s and early 1970s saw a rise in a 'free school' movement (very different in meaning from the UK Coalition government's twenty-first century definition of a 'free school' in England), where increasingly libertarian approaches to school management and curriculum choices were prevalent. But the 1970s also saw a major economic upheaval largely associated with a sharp escalation in oil prices. It was in 1976 that the then Prime Minister James Callaghan, in a speech at Ruskin College, famously articulated concern about educational standards and there was a move towards increased central control of the curriculum (and later of teaching).

That year also saw a famous cause célèbre in the shape of one primary school in north London, William Tyndale, where the teaching staff had apparently handed over considerable control to the pupils in the running of the school. Following a range of complaints by parents which were picked up in the popular media, the local authority, the Inner London Educational Authority, which itself was often depicted as left-wing and progressive, set up an inquiry. In due course this led to the removal of the bulk of the teaching staff and the reining in of the radical practices that had been adopted. The influence of this case went way beyond the particular school and tended to fuel a widespread anxiety that many primary schools were failing their children in teaching the basics of literacy and numeracy and were disorganised and chaotic.

There was an escalating 'moral panic' about such matters, fuelled by such publications as 'The Black Papers', a series of essays criticising the educational establishment for its alleged failures to deliver what was needed by young people and indeed by the country at large. The extent to which primary education was being shaped by the press and by politicians increased further during the 1980s both in spite of and because of some of the most extensive empirical studies of what was actually happening in primary schools. The 'ORACLE' study, first published in 1980 (Galton *et al.*, 1980), actually revealed that there was remarkably little evidence of child-centred approaches and indeed that there was very little real collaborative group work going on in primary schools. Indeed primary classrooms remained dominated by teacher talk and by whole-class teaching. Just four years later, a study by Bennett (1984) sought to link teaching styles with pupil progress. In spite of there again being very little evidence of wholehearted progressive approaches, this study was seized upon by sections of the media as demonstrating that 'informal' methods did not work well. In fact, Bennett's study showed that the very best learning (pupil progress) occurred in situations that were informal but where the teaching was of unusually high calibre. In other words the actual findings of the study were somewhat ambiguous, indeed intriguing, but they were greatly simplified in the way they were reported in much of the media and thereby added more fuel to the anti-progressive fire that was being stoked by press and politicians.

Historian Brian Simon (1991), reviewing these developments, described these shifts as 'swings', with the metaphorical allusion being to a pendulum. As we shall now see, the return swing was not long in coming.

Government takes control – from 1988

This backlash against progressivism was therefore somewhat strange, in that it was a backlash against a particular representation of primary education rather than against what research actually showed to be happening. Nevertheless fuelled by such concerns and encouraged by continuing reporting of low literacy (and numeracy) levels, the scene was set for a major intervention in the curriculum by the government. Indeed the curriculum was just one part of the major intervention in English education policy that was the Education Reform Act of 1988. This had been launched as a Parliamentary Bill in 1987 by Margaret Thatcher's Secretary of State for Education, Kenneth Baker. As well as introducing radical reforms in curriculum and assessment across the compulsory school age range, the Bill and subsequent Act also made provision for radical changes to the management and governance of schools, including provision for schools to 'opt out' of local government control and for successful schools to expand through 'open enrolment'.

Without doubt this was the biggest shake-up of schooling in England, Wales and Northern Ireland since 1944. Furthermore the 1944 Act had specified very little about the school curriculum, it being generally assumed that this was a matter largely for local authorities and teachers. The only curriculum area that had been laid down in compulsory fashion at that time had been religious education.

The National Curriculum that was introduced covered the compulsory school range and was laid out in 14 subjects with hundreds of attainment targets being set out within each one, within a number of 'levels'.

The core subjects were:

- English
- mathematics
- science.

The original foundation subjects were:

- art and design
- design and technology
- geography
- history
- information and communication technology
- modern foreign languages
- music
- personal, social and health education
- physical education.

Religious education was also a requirement as was sex education. The subject of citizenship was added later, but was not to be a separate subject within the primary curriculum.

Alongside the curriculum, new national testing arrangements were introduced including tests for all pupils at the ages of seven, 11 and 13. The tests affecting the primary school were therefore at the respective conclusion of each key stage. They were called Standard Assessment Tasks or SATs and were developed in the three 'core' subjects, English, mathematics and science. The results of the tests were to be made publicly available on a school basis, so that this could be used by parents as one factor in deciding which school they might wish to send their child to. The results of the KS2 tests at the age of 11 were also to be sent through with each child to the secondary school to which they were transferring, in order to help with decisions to be made there about setting or streaming. In the remaining 'foundation' subjects, there were no national tests although teachers were expected to make their own assessments of how children were faring. Indeed teachers were expected to make their own assessments of each child across the full range of subjects at the end of every school year, not just at the end of the key stages.

Prior to these developments practices relating to assessment, testing and transfer had been determined locally. The so-called '11-plus' exam taken in the final year of primary school, as a means of determining which pupils might enter grammar schools, had gradually faded out in most areas as secondary provision became increasingly comprehensive. Practices associated with children's transfer from primary to secondary school were varied across the country. Indeed, part of the fundamental rationale for introducing a national curriculum and national testing was that there was far too much variation in practice across the country and it was therefore not possible, or at least was very difficult, for teachers or parents in one part of the country to make comparisons with outcomes in other parts of the country and also made it problematic for children if they were moving from one area to another.

In Wales and Northern Ireland, broadly similar arrangements were introduced, albeit with some curricular differences such as the inclusion of Welsh language provision or, in Northern Ireland, the inclusion of different cross-curricular themes such as 'education for mutual understanding'. Scottish primary schools were not covered by the Education Reform Act although, through the Scottish Office, the government did attempt to introduce a number of the structural measures. Curriculum was developed through the creation of Curriculum Guidelines 5–14 which did bear some similarities to the English National Curriculum, for example in introducing levels of attainment and in being strongly subject based. However these guidelines were just that, and schools and teachers could – at least in theory – decide on the extent to which they would actually adopt them. Testing arrangements were also put in place but were much more concerned with providing progress data on individual children, rather than providing data for the purpose of comparing schools.

There was considerable consternation expressed by teachers and their organisation in England in response to the National Curriculum proposals. A fierce debate ensued for several months but the central elements of the policy were passed into law during 1988 and a programme of implementation was put in place. The main concerns of teachers centred on the level of detail in the prescribed curriculum, the fears that it would actually be the tests that would determine the curriculum as taught and the sheer 'overload' that such a cumbersome scheme would create. There would be little scope for topic-based teaching or of curriculum integration, it was feared. But underlying much of this reaction was a concern among teachers that their very professional identity was under assault. It was clear that no longer was the child to be at the centre of the primary school, rather it was to be curriculum content which dominated.

Key questions for reflection

To what extent should the primary school curriculum be determined at a national level?

How different would you expect the curriculum to be in each of the four nations of the UK?

Although major adaptations were made over the following years (a review led by Sir Ron Dearing was established within three years) the major planks of the structures remained in place. The 1990s was then a period when primary teachers were having to make major adjustments in their approaches and this was the cause of much disquiet and discomfort for many teachers as has been found in a number of research studies (Osborn *et al.*, 2000; Menter *et al.*, 1997). However there was also considerable evidence that the new curricular and testing regimes were causing children themselves some anxiety and, in some cases, stress (Pollard *et al.*, 1994).

Given the complexity of the National Curriculum in England it is perhaps not surprising that the question of subject knowledge became dominant again during the 1990s. In 1992, the then Secretary of State for Education established a group of experts, who became know as the 'Three Wise Men' to advise him on Curriculum Organisation and Classroom Practice in Primary Schools. Their report (Alexander *et al.*, 1992) did suggest that there should be increased subject differentiation at least in the upper years of primary schooling and also that teachers working at these stages might need further training and development in order to be able to support such a curriculum. Furthermore, the review commented on teaching methods, raising renewed interest in whole-class teaching as being as important as group or individually based approaches.

In some ways this was one of the forerunners for subsequent developments. If 1988 had seen an unprecedented government intervention in the curriculum, it was only ten years later that we saw a very significant intervention into teaching itself. This indeed had strong links with the curriculum. During the 1990s there was increasing reference to data in the form of test results, both because they were now much more available but also under the influence of global developments. There had been a steady expansion in the deployment of international assessment systems, such as PISA (Programme for International Student Assessment), PIRLS (Progress in International Reading Survey) and TIMSS (Trends in International Mathematics and Science Study). All of these international schemes facilitated comparison of education success between countries. With politicians increasingly making assertions about the need for a successful 'knowledge economy', when there were few visible improvements in levels of literacy and numeracy, and alleged evidence that England was 'slipping down' the international league tables, the scene was set for more radical policy development.

When the Labour Party was elected to power at Westminster in 1997, following 18 years of Conservative governments, it was on the back of incoming Prime Minister Tony Blair's famous 'three priorities': 'Education, Education, Education'. The previous government had been developing plans for major initiatives for literacy and numeracy but it was the new government that fully developed and then rapidly implemented 'national strategies' for literacy and numeracy. At the core of these were requirements for primary school teachers to include 'a literacy hour' and 'a numeracy hour' in each school day. The pattern of these hours was set out and included particular teaching methods. A huge training programme was instigated in order that these approaches were adopted and increasing attention was then given to children's test results in English and maths. Schools (and teachers), where results were not improving, were identified and singled out for special attention. This was partly done through the inspection process that itself had been considerably tightened up since 1992 when the Office for Standards in Education (Ofsted) was created to manage these processes.

Although there were similar concerns about levels of literacy and numeracy in Scotland, such an approach was not adopted there. However, one of the incoming Labour government's other key policy areas was devolution and by the turn of the century/ millennium, new devolved administration had been established in the three smaller jurisdictions of Northern Ireland, Scotland and Wales (although the Northern Ireland Assembly did not operate continuously in the early stages). There was at this time a formal devolution of power in respect of education policy, and so we began to see increasing divergence in Wales and Northern Ireland, while the earlier divergence in Scotland was consolidated. Literacy and numeracy strategies were, therefore, not as rigidly developed in Northern Ireland and Wales. The smaller countries also began to remove some of the testing arrangements, which were felt to be over-burdensome and unhelpful, as well as the constraints of the National Curriculum, and to develop more distinctive approaches in each jurisdiction. The primary curriculum consulted upon in Northern Ireland in 2002, and implemented from 2007, for example, introduced a distinct Foundation Stage and moved towards stronger integration of subjects and much greater flexibility in content in the other two key stages, for example, by combining subjects such as geography, history and science into a more child-friendly area of study entitled 'The World Around Us'. Thematic approaches to primary teaching and learning are strongly encouraged and supported by illustrative thematic units of work, with a strong emphasis on inquiry and the development of higher-order thinking skills and personal capabilities. The revised curriculum aim of empowering young people to make informed choices and decisions throughout their lives as individuals and as contributors to society, the economy and environment, was later to be mirrored in subsequent curriculum reform in Scotland. So too was the stronger emphasis on the early years as a distinct phase, an emphasis which was given even greater priority and status within Welsh curriculum reforms. More detail on these developments is provided in Chapter 3.

During the first decade of the twenty-first century, the emphasis on a subject-based curriculum with priority given to basic skills, measured through tightly controlled assessment systems, became embedded in England, if less so elsewhere in the UK. However, there were increasing concerns that the approach being taken was not producing the results that were desired. There were calls from the traditional side for even greater prescription and control, while there were calls from the progressive and developmental side for greater relaxation and for increased responsibility to be given to teachers in making curricular and assessment decisions. However it has to be said that this apparent binary division was not always clear and there were some concerns shared by commentators of many persuasions.

It was against this backdrop that what became known as The Cambridge Primary Review was set up. This was to be a three-year independent inquiry into the state of primary education in England led by one of the leading primary education researchers, Professor Robin Alexander at the University of Cambridge. The review was funded by a charity, the Esmee Fairbairn Foundation, and commissioned a wide range of research reports and conducted numerous consultation meetings across the country that brought in the experiences of teachers, parents and children and led, in 2010, to the publication of a report *Children, their World, their Education* (Alexander, 2010). However this report was not the only output from the Review. Over its duration various research reports had been published as well as interim reports on the emerging findings. Rather than welcoming these contributions the then government sought to distance itself from the investigation, indeed it appeared to use sophisticated 'spin' tactics in an attempt to discredit the Review. It also set up its own curriculum review under a former senior inspector of schools, Jim (later Sir Jim) Rose. It is not without irony that Rose and Alexander had been two of the three so-called 'wise men' who an earlier Conservative administration had commissioned to review the organisation and management of the primary curriculum (Sir Chris Woodhead, who became Chief Inspector of Schools at Ofsted, was the third).

The Rose Report was published not long before the conclusion of the Cambridge Review final report, again in an apparent attempt to 'spoil' the dissemination of the latter. Plans were put in place by government to introduce changes based on recommendations in the Rose Report, including a 'simplification' of the curriculum. However in May 2010 a new government was elected, a Conservative–Liberal democratic coalition, with Michael Gove appointed as Education Secretary. One of Gove's early actions was to suspend the programme arising from Rose and then subsequently to establish his own curriculum review.

There were similar anxieties about the curriculum guidance in Scotland and, following a National Debate on education priorities, the Scottish Executive (later the Scottish Government) drew up proposals to reshape the curriculum across the full range from 3–18 around four capacities that learners were intended to develop as:

- successful learners
- confident individuals
- responsible citizens
- effective contributors.

These four capacities underlay the proposals for '*Curriculum for Excellence*' which was published in 2003 and has been implemented from 2010 onwards. The policy is laid out as 'Experiences and Outcomes' in each of eight curriculum areas:

- expressive arts
- health and wellbeing
- languages
- mathematics
- religious and moral education
- sciences
- social studies
- technologies.

A restructuring of assessment is currently proceeding in Scotland alongside the curriculum reforms. The Curriculum for Excellence is defined in terms of 'Experiences and Outcomes' that learners are entitled to encounter during their schooling. One of the intentions behind this reform was to create more flexibility in the curriculum allowing for greater local determination and responsiveness than there had been with Curriculum 5–14. One of the specific goals of the reform had been to 'declutter the primary curriculum', the view being taken that too much 'content' had been accrued and that this was making the task of teaching unmanageable.

The response of teachers to this new-found autonomy was in fact mixed, at least at the early stages of the developments. Although primary teachers were generally more enthusiastic and welcoming of this development than secondary teachers, nevertheless there were many calls for greater specification, more exemplification, anxiety about assessment and inspection. All of this did lead to the development of more detailed curriculum materials being published by the government than had originally been intended.

So we see again that current provision is but the outcome of a continuing process of development. We should not see the primary curriculum as being fixed, but rather as the present manifestation of a continuously evolving debate about what it is that younger children should be learning, in terms of knowledge and concepts, skills and dispositions. This debate reflects changing priorities in society and changing views about the relationship between primary schooling and what precedes and succeeds it, that is provision for the early years and secondary school provision respectively.

What can be learned from elsewhere? Teachers and the primary curriculum

As we reviewed the development of the primary school curriculum over the past 100 years or more we have mentioned some of the differences that have occurred within the UK, between the different jurisdictions. These have been interesting and have given some indication of how national culture and politics may influence the school curriculum. Having suggested from the outset that the primary curriculum does have distinctively British origins, in this section of the chapter we want to reflect rather more widely and offer some insights into the features that emerge when the British primary curricula as compared with those beyond these isles.

In a five-country study reported in 2000, again by Alexander, it is suggested that the primary curriculum is much more a matter of debate and challenge in England and the United States than it is in Russia, India or France (Alexander, 2000). His analysis suggests that while there are common subject areas in the primary school curriculum their relative weighting varies significantly and there are some interesting English idiosyncrasies. The English curriculum, especially by comparison with the French, is driven by concerns about the economy and employment. England is the only nation where numeracy is given equal billing to literacy, and indeed there is little attention given to spoken language by comparison with several other countries. Other curricula are constructed with a much greater eye on civil society and citizenship. So, for example, the primary curriculum in France is based on a core of French, history, geography and civic education. Alexander also points out that England is almost unique (and is unique in Europe) in not including the teaching of a foreign language in its requirements for primary education.

Indeed, Alexander sees the firm imposition of a national curriculum in 1988 as running counter to the long-standing tradition of teacher determination of what is taught:

> when the National Curriculum was summarily imposed by the Thatcher government in 1987–8 in the teeth of professional opposition, not only was it widely condemned as an affront to professional autonomy and local democracy, but the government's behaviour also guaranteed that education professionals would continue to resist long after the proposals became law, especially as the government's railroading tactics set the style for their subsequent handling of national curriculum matters.
>
> (Alexander, 2000, pp. 549–50)

There was however considerable wider support for the introduction of a national curriculum, including that of many parents and their organisations, as well as some members of the education professions themselves.

Conclusion

Primary education in the UK today is clearly very different from the elementary education that was offered at the start of the twentieth century. However there are some elements in what emerged as primary education in the later parts of that century that had echoes of that earlier approach. Indeed in some ways, as the tightening grip of government took hold again, in the last decade of the twentieth century and since, there was some sense of a return to those priorities. At that time – and especially in England – we saw a strong emphasis on basic skills and a strongly subject-based curriculum. We also saw a system that gave little autonomy to teachers in making decisions about what to teach and even about how to teach it.

So the elementary tradition is clearly still there and some would argue that the preparatory tradition is also there. This is seen in the emphasis on subjects and certainly there continues to be much concern about the links between primary and secondary schools – do primary schools actually prepare students for the next stage and how are the transition arrangements managed in order to ensure maximum continuity? Many reports suggest that students tend to 'platform' (level out) or even regress in their attainment in the first year or two of secondary education.

But what of the developmental tradition? Well, this account has suggested that it never took as strong a hold on practice as was often suggested, even if it did influence the thinking and professional identity of many primary teachers. In many people's minds, child-centredness has 'developed a bad name', not least because it is alleged to have failed many children, especially some of those living in the most challenging circumstances. However, the need to respond to children's individual development does sometimes still appear, for example through such concepts as 'personalised learning' as well as in concepts and practices associated with 'differentiation' (for more on such notions see Chapter 4). The other field in which one can see some legacy of the developmental tradition is in the resurgence interest in creativity within the curriculum (see Chapter 9 for more about these aspects). This is demonstrated through a number of official initiatives (many initiated following the publication of the Robinson report on creativity, see NACCCE, 1999) as well as in the attraction for some parents of schools that emphasise these aspects of learning, such as the (private) Waldorf schools based on the ideas of Rudolf Steiner.

Key questions for reflection

In current primary provision in the part of the UK where you live, how do you see the current balance between the elementary, preparatory and developmental/ progressive traditions in the primary schools that you know? Where is this balance determined – nationally, regionally or in the school itself?

> What should 11-year-old children be able to do, to know and understand, when they transfer into secondary school?

What does the future hold for primary education? On the basis of this review of its history perhaps the one thing that one could anticipate with some certainty is that it will continue to change and develop. It remains a crucial phase of education within the UK and beyond, because it serves the key function of being the site of children learning the skills without which their subsequent learning will be severely hampered. And it prepares children for their subsequent experience of schooling in larger institutions. If secondary education goes through radical changes in the future, perhaps through greater reliance on virtual learning environments and other technological developments, it does seem possible that this will have effects on the provision of primary education. Or on the other hand if interventions in the early years (i.e. pre-primary) are successfully sustained, given the widespread recognition of these early stages in shaping children's futures, how might primary education be reshaped in response? It will remain fascinating to see how the three traditions outlined in this chapter rise and fall in 'the mix' and to see how teachers' work, professionalism and identities change over the years ahead.

Teacher education task

Discuss the purposes of primary education. What do you think they are and which groups of people do you think should have a say in establishing what they are and how the curriculum should be constructed? For example, what part should be played in determining these matters by, respectively, teachers, researchers, government ministers, government officials, parents, faith organisations, pressure groups or other possible 'stakeholders'?

Further reading

The seminal and defining document on primary education in England and Wales is undoubtedly the Plowden Report (Plowden, 1967). Even though much has changed since its publication, it remains a very important reference point by which to gauge contemporary practice.

On a similar scale, but indeed providing a much more contemporary perspective is the Cambridge Primary Review (Alexander, 2010). The final report and recommendations are well worth studying and indeed comparing with the Plowden Report.

In order to get a deeper understanding of the history and politics of primary education in the UK, Cunningham's text (Cunningham, 2012) in the same series as the current book is extremely valuable.

References

Alexander, R. (2000) *Culture and Pedagogy: International Comparisons in Primary Education.* Oxford: Blackwell.

Alexander, R. (ed.) (2010) *Children, their World, their Education: Final Report and Recommendations of the Cambridge Primary Review.* London: Routledge.

Alexander, R., Rose, J. and Woodhead, C. (1992) *Curriculum Organisation and Classroom Practice in Primary Schools: A Discussion Paper.* London: DES.

Bennett, N. (1984) *Teaching Styles and Pupil Porgress.* London: Open Books.

Blyth, W. (1965) *English Primary Education: A Sociological Description.* London: Routledge and Kegan Paul.

Cunningham, P. (2012) *Politics and the Primary Teacher.* London: Routledge.

Galton, M., Simon, B. and Croll, P. (1980) *Inside the Primary Classroom.* London: Routledge and Kegan Paul.

Menter, I., Muschamp, Y., Nicholls, P., Ozga, J. and Pollard, A. (1997) *Work and Identity in the Primary School.* Buckingham: Open University Press.

Ministry of Education (1958) *Primary Education (Suggestions for the Consideration of Teachers and Others Concerned with the Work of Primary Schools).* London: HMSO.

National Advisory Committee on Creative and Cultural Education (NACCCE) (1999) *All Our Futures: Creativity, Culture and Education.* Suffolk: DfEE Publications.

Osborn, M., McNess, E. and Broadfoot, P. (2000) *What Teachers Do: Changing Policy and Practice in Primary Education.* London: Continuum.

Plowden, Lady (1967) *Children and their Primary Schools.* London: HMSO.

Pollard, A., Broadfoot, P., Croll, P. and Osborn, M. (1994) *Changing English Primary Schools: The Impact of the Education Reform Act at Key Stage 1.* London: Cassell.

Simon, B. (1991) *Education and the Social Order.* London: Lawrence and Wishart.

Chapter 3

Aims and objectives

Carmel Gallagher and Dominic Wyse

Chapter summary

This chapter explores national curriculum aims in England, Northern Ireland, Scotland and Wales. The chapter shows that the curriculum and its aims can be understood, structured and implemented in significantly different ways. Our thinking has been informed by two main lines of theory. The first line of theory comes from a philosophical understanding of the limitations of *rationalism*. Rationalism is represented in the chapter as the imposition of particular models of curricula on teachers and pupils by nation states, particularly objectives-led curricula. The second line of thinking underpinning the chapter is the categorisation of curricula as one of three main emphases: i) content-driven curricula; ii) objectives-driven curricula; iii) process-driven curricula.

The chapter begins with a direct comparison of the national curriculum aims in the four countries, some explanation of their history, and some reflections on their key features. This is followed by a brief account of the way in which the curriculum is underpinned by views of the nature of knowledge. Finally we consider one of the most influential rationalist models, the objectives-driven model. We conclude with possible improvements for the development of curriculum aims in future.

Alec stands in front of the interactive whiteboard ready to begin the lesson. He reminds the class that they are going to write an account of yesterday's trip to the local castle. The children are encouraged to share their recollections. They remember with excitement the walk through the castle's dungeons. One of the children compares the smell of the dungeons to his dog when it has been swimming in a local stream. Alec is genuinely enthused by the children's reflections. He is naturally tempted to build on their excitement by exploring 'tales from the dungeons' in an open-ended way that could lead to a range of writing. But he knows that the school's scheme of work, building on the national curriculum, requires him to teach the features of the 'recount genre' that lesson.

Alec explains to the children the kinds of things they need to demonstrate in their writing by showing them a 'model' piece of writing from a government recommended resource. Next he asks a child to read the objectives for the lesson that he has written on the whiteboard in child-friendly language.

Alec: Right can someone read the objectives for the lesson?
Sarah: To be able to write a recount
Alec: And the next?
Chamak: To use words and phrases to interest the reader.
Alec: Good, last objective?
Sinead: Make sure that the necessary information is included.

Alec reminds them that they must write the lesson objectives in their exercise books. After a check to ensure the children are clear about the task Alex asks them to go to their tables and start work.

In this example at least two types of aims are evident. The first type is the teacher's aims for the lesson. The short-term lesson objectives are prepared by the teacher in advance of the lesson. The objectives are made clear to the pupils who have to write them in their exercise books. The focus of the lesson is driven by the objectives. This has become common practice, but the key question we must ask in the context of this chapter is, why has this become common practice, and what is the evidence that this is effective and appropriate?

The other type of aim, which does not come to fruition in the lesson, is more subtle. Alec's enthusiasm for the children's interests, expressed in their excitement about the castle dungeons, is tied in with his beliefs about how children learn, and his theories of education. Alec's view is that teaching should enable children to make choices in their learning. He believes that when children make choices they are often more motivated, and that higher motivation leads to better outcomes. Imagine if the lesson had proceeded like this:

Alec stands in front of the interactive whiteboard ready to begin the lesson. He reminds the class that they are going to write an account of yesterday's trip to the local castle. The children are encouraged to share their recollections. They remember with excitement the walk through the castle's dungeons. One of the children compares the smell of the dungeons to his dog when it has been swimming in a local stream. Another child remembers a scary film with a scene in a dungeon where a man is chained to the wall. Eager to contribute, more and more of the children's hands go up. At one point the discussion turns to whether ghosts really exist.

After ten minutes of intense and lively discussion Alec decides to abandon the lesson on the recount genre.

Alec: Right children, I think that our class book 'Tales from the Dungeons' is long overdue. Let's think about how we are going to write it . . .

The examples of a lesson hint at two different ways to think about the curriculum and its aims. The first example we might call an *objectives-led* teaching approach. The second example we might call a *child-centred* approach (or developmental approach, as described in Chapter 2). These different approaches encourage us to think about the nature of aims, and their impact on teachers and pupils. They prompt the question, what are appropriate aims for a curriculum?

This chapter explores national curriculum aims in England, Northern Ireland, Scotland and Wales, and the 'Common Curriculum' aims in Northern Ireland. The chapter shows that the curriculum and its aims can be understood, structured and implemented in significantly different ways. Our thinking has been informed by two main lines of theory. The first line of theory comes from a philosophical understanding of the limitations of *rationalism*. Rationalism is represented in the chapter as the imposition of particular models of curricula on teachers and pupils by nation states, particularly objectives-led curricula. An alternative to rationalism are the ideas of *technical reason* and *practical reason*, that were first addressed by the ancient Greek philosopher Aristotle (Dunne, 1993). Technical reason and practical reason are represented by a more subtle understanding of the way that teachers work as professionals and the ways that they make decisions.

The second line of thinking underpinning the chapter is the categorisation of curricula as one of three main emphases: i) content-driven curricula; ii) objectives-driven curricula; and iii) process-driven curricula (Kelly, 2009; Ross, 2000). These categories are not mutually exclusive but they are useful ways to describe different approaches to curriculum planning.

The chapter begins with a direct comparison of the aims of the 'national' curriculum in each of the four countries, some explanation of their history, and some reflections on their key features. This is followed by a brief account of the way in which the curriculum is underpinned by views of the nature of knowledge. Finally we consider one of the most influential rationalist models, the objectives-driven model. We conclude with recommendations for the development of curriculum aims in future.

The aims of UK national curricula

The highest level of national curriculum requirements is expressed in aims for the whole curriculum, which are intended to capture its overall purpose and outcomes. For example, the aspiration to encourage pupils to become lifelong learners; to become good citizens; to acquire the skills needed for employment; to develop as creative thinkers, etc.

Before we compare the aims in the different countries it is important to signal that the reason we have national curricula at all is as a result of particular laws enacted by governments. In the UK prior to 1988 teachers, schools and pupils had much more freedom over their curricula (see Chapter 2; and for a longer account of the history and politics, see Cunningham, 2011). For example, when the authors began teaching there was no national curriculum. The planning for each half term was often centred on a theme or topic (chosen by the teachers and school) in addition to some separate subject teaching, particularly of maths and English. However, in 1988 a new law called The Education Reform Act (ERA) was enacted. For the first time this law gave power to the Minister for Education to establish a national curriculum. The aims for the curriculum described in the ERA are called *general requirements*.

(1) The curriculum for a maintained school or maintained nursery school satisfies the requirements of this section [of the act] if it is a balanced and broadly based curriculum which –

(a) promotes the spiritual, moral, cultural, mental and physical development of pupils at the school and of society, and

(b) prepares pupils at the school for the opportunities, responsibilities and experiences of later life.

These requirements covered England and Wales. Northern Ireland also adopted them as part of the Education Reform (Northern Ireland) Order 1989. Scotland did not have the same requirements. In Scotland the Education (Scotland) Act 1980 very clearly gave power over the curriculum to local authorities: '(2) In any such school the education authority shall have *the sole power* of regulating the curriculum and of appointing teachers' (The Education (Scotland) Act 1980, Section 21, p. 13, emphasis added). So it is important to note from the start that Scotland and Northern Ireland did not legally place the power to establish a national curriculum directly in the hands of a minister, something that is an important reflection of the different ways their curricula developed as you will see as this chapter progresses.

The first national curricula in England, Wales and Northern Ireland represented, according to some, a mismatch between a cultural transmission model (which fails to question absolutist views of knowledge and uncontested views of culture) and a rationalist model (which ignores these questions and claims to be 'value-neutral') (Kelly, 2009, p. 89). Kelly draws attention to the failure of those responsible for constructing the curriculum to appreciate the conceptual differences between these two models. In his view the outcome represented the worst of both worlds, reducing education to a 'delivery' model where teachers were no longer required to think about their purposes or objectives, and where they no longer had the freedom to select content according to the interests and needs of their pupils.

Key questions for reflection

In what ways might teachers influence the development of new national curricula?

To what extent do you consider it appropriate, or otherwise, for a minister to have direct control over the detail of national curricula?

In England concerns emerged over a period of years that the general requirements did not provide sufficient clarity of purpose. As a result the Qualifications and Curriculum Authority (QCA) commissioned an analysis of curriculum aims across 20 countries which showed that the curriculum aims in many countries had aspects in common. The report argued that, 'In an ideal world, national values which are clearly understood and shared by all, form a coherent thread which permeates the education system from aims through to outcomes in clear steps' (Le Métais, 1997, p. 3). On the basis of these recommendations the QCA developed a three-page elaborated statement of aims, values and purposes for the curriculum in England which was inserted as a non-statutory preface in the National Curriculum Handbook of 2000. The elaborated aims were:

Aim 1: The school curriculum should aim to provide opportunities for all pupils to learn and to achieve.

Aim 2: The school curriculum should aim to promote pupils' spiritual, moral, social and cultural development and prepare all pupils for the opportunities, responsibilities and experiences of life.

Aim 2 subsumed the 'general requirements' from the ERA but Aim 1 was new, reflecting an emphasis on improving *standards* (a key word in the New Labour government's policies from 1997 to 2010) through a stronger focus on learning and achievement. The statement of aims was developed after the curriculum had already been reviewed and thus did not influence curriculum structures and subject requirements in the way that Le Métais envisaged.

In 2008–9, in England, three reviews of the primary curriculum were undertaken. The first of these, the independent Cambridge Primary Review, proposed 12 new aims for the primary curriculum, clustered under three headings as follows:

- **The Individual:** Well-being; Engagement; Empowerment; Autonomy.
- **Self, others and the wider world;** Encouragement, respect and reciprocity; Promoting interdependence and sustainability; Empowering local, national and global citizenship; Celebrating culture and community.
- **Learning, knowing and doing:** Exploring, knowing, understanding and making sense; Fostering Skill; Exciting imagination; Enacting dialogue.

At the same time the New Labour government commissioned a review of the national curriculum by Sir Jim Rose. Less well known was the year-long inquiry led by the House of Commons Education Committee. One of the conclusions of this committee was as follows:

111. One recommendation of the Rose Review interim report is that the primary curriculum should follow the new secondary curriculum in terms of being underpinned by a statutory set of aims. Furthermore, it suggests that the statement of aims for the secondary curriculum 'holds good for the primary phase, and indeed for the [Early Years Foundation Stage]', and requests comments about the statement's suitability in this regard. We believe that, as well as considering the appropriateness of the secondary curriculum statement of aims for the primary curriculum and the Early Years Foundation Stage, the Rose Review should consider the potential to apply the statement to 14–19 provision also.

(House of Commons, 2009, p. 37)

This was an unfortunate recommendation in a generally outstanding report, and one that is further evidence of policy borrowing. The simple adoption of aims developed for the secondary curriculum (see below) for primary and early years fails to allow for consideration of the developmental differences between children at the different phases. It also reflects a trend in national curriculum development of pressures from requirements for older pupils impacting on the requirements for younger pupils. Contrary to the committee's proposal there is a strong logic to the idea that national curriculum should build from the needs of the youngest children upwards. Even more serious than the developmental arguments, this recommendation forecloses consultation about aims for the primary curriculum. However, in the end the Conservative–Liberal Democrat coalition government which came into office in 2010 rejected all such proposals in setting up yet another review of the national curriculum in England.

In Northern Ireland between 2000 and 2003 an extensive review of 'The Common Curriculum' paid significant attention to the aims of the curriculum. The revised Northern Ireland Curriculum, implemented from 2007 onwards, was reorganised under one overarching aim and three objectives to provide opportunities for young people to develop as individuals and as contributors to society, the economy and the environment (see Figure 3.1, Council for the Curriculum Examinations and Assessment, 2007).

The Education (Scotland) Act 2000 legislated that, 'education should be directed to the development of the personality, talents, and mental and physical abilities of the child or young person to their fullest potential' and that 'due regard, so far as is reasonably practicable, should be paid to the views of the child or young person in decisions that significantly affect them, taking account of the child or young person's age and maturity'. This underpins an increasing emphasis by the policy makers in Scotland to seek the views of young people and involve them in discussions about curriculum development and implementation. Scotland's national debate on education in 2002 was the starting point for the development of a Curriculum for Excellence (CfE). Unlike the other nations of the UK (that have separate requirements for different stages, ages or phases) the CfE applies to all pupils/students from age three to age 19. Scotland's curriculum aims are expressed as 'four capacities' (see Figure 3.2 (Scottish Government, 2011, online)) which aspire 'to enable young people to become: successful learners; confident individuals; responsible citizens; effective contributors' (Scottish Government, 2011, online).

Drawing on curriculum developments in Northern Ireland and Scotland, the national curriculum aims for Key Stage 3 in England were substantially revised again in 2007 (Figure 3.3; Qualifications and Curriculum Development Authority, 2009).

Wales' education system and its national curriculum changed significantly once Wales become devolved from England in 1998. The School Curriculum for Wales was implemented in a staged way from 2008 to 2011/12. It included a longer early years phase than any of the other nation states (age three to age seven). The curriculum in Wales had been revised in the context of a broad vision for education and lifelong learning (see Figure 3.4; Department for Children, Education, Lifelong Learning and Skills, 2008).

Uniquely, these seven core aims for education in Wales as a 'Learning Country' are set in the 'broader context of [a] vision for children and young people overall'. This idea was seen in England in the New Labour government's *Children's Plan* and associated *Every Child Matters* (ECM) initiatives, but not included specifically in the national curriculum (although the Key Stage 3 'Big Picture of the Curriculum' made links to these broader

WHOLE CURRICULUM AIM AND OBJECTIVES

Aim

The Northern Ireland Curriculum aims to empower young people to develop their potential and to make informed and responsible choices and decisions throughout their lives.

Objectives

The learning opportunities provided through the Northern Ireland Curriculum should help young people to develop as:

Individuals	Contributors to Society	Contributors to the Economy and Environment
Throughout the primary stages teachers should help children to: • develop self-confidence, self-esteem and self-discipline; • understand their own and others' feelings and emotions; • develop the ability to talk about how they feel; • develop their motivation to learn and their individual creative potential; • listen to and interact positively with others; • explore and understand how others live; **(Personal and Mutual Understanding)** • have an understanding of healthy eating and the importance of exercise; • develop positive attitudes towards an active and healthy lifestyle, relationships, personal growth and change; • become aware of key issues which affect their physical, social and mental well-being and that of others; • develop an awareness of their own personal safety; **(Personal Health)** • develop an awareness of right and wrong; • develop an awareness of how their actions can affect others; • understand that values, choices and decisions should be informed by a sense of fairness; • take responsibility for their actions; • develop tolerance and mutual respect for others; **(Moral Character)** • develop a sense of awe and wonder about the world around them. **(Spiritual Understanding)**	Throughout the primary stages teachers should help children to: • become aware of some of their rights and responsibilities; • become aware of some of the issues and problems in society; • contribute to creating a better world for those around them; **(Citizenship)** • develop an awareness and respect for: - the different lifestyles of others; - similarities and differences in families and people in the wider community; • understand some of their own and others' cultural traditions; • be aware of how we rely on each other; **(Cultural Understanding)** • be aware of, and use, information available to us through all sorts of media; • become aware of the potential impact of media in influencing our personal views, choices and decisions; **(Media Awareness)** • become aware of the imbalances in the world around us, at both a local and a global level; • become aware of the potential impact of developments upon the lives of others. **(Ethical Awareness)**	Throughout the primary stages teachers should help children to: • develop literacy, numeracy and ICT skills; • develop their aptitudes, abilities and creativity; • be willing to expand their learning and performance throughout their lives; • work independently and as a member of a team; • develop perseverance, initiative and flexibility; • be willing to take calculated risks when appropriate; • use critical and creative thinking to solve problems and make decisions; • identify the main reasons why people set up their own business. **(Employability)** • learn to manage their money and build up savings; • interpret information in order to make informed choices as consumers; • develop an understanding of the importance of using resources carefully in the classroom; • develop an awareness of some environmental issues; **(Economic Awareness)** • appreciate the environment and their role in maintaining and improving it; • understand how actions can affect the environment. **(Education for Sustainable Development)**

Figure 3.1 Northern Ireland curriculum aims.

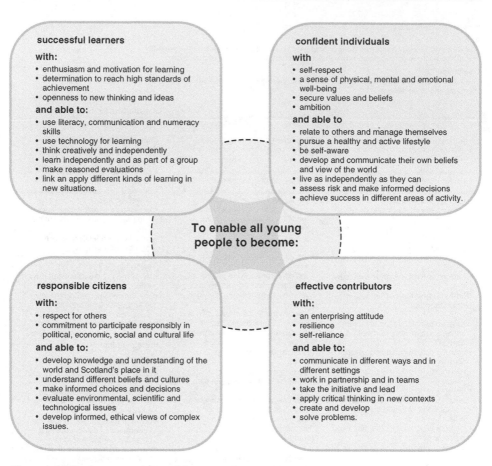

Figure 3.2 The four 'capacities' of the Scottish Curriculum for Excellence.

policies). The second major difference is that Wales' aims are developed from the United Nations Convention on the Rights of the Child (UN CRC). The framing of national curricula in children's rights terms is a radical one, and a far cry from the top-down approach adopted in England since 1988. The recognition of children's rights can be seen to a lesser degree in the commitment made in Scotland to seek the views of young people and involve them in discussions about curriculum development and implementation. While explicit mention of the UN CRC is not evident in Northern Ireland policy documents, nevertheless, a seven-year cohort study was undertaken there between 1996 and 2002, formally seeking the views of over 3,000 young people aged 10–18 about their curriculum experiences (Harland *et al.*, 2002). Their feedback was then taken into account in the revisions of the curriculum.

To sum up this comparison of the aims in the four countries, you can see that the aims of England's revised secondary curriculum are almost identical to Scotland's four capacities, which, in turn, reflect the substance of the Northern Ireland aims. Northern Ireland's revised aims drew on aspects of the three-page English aims of 2000. It may or may not be significant that the smaller countries went through more extensive public

The curriculum should enable all young people to become:
- **successful learners** who enjoy learning, make progress and achieve
- **confident individuals** who are able to live safe, healthy and fulfilling lives
- **responsible citizens** who make a positive contribution to society.

Successful learners who . . .	Confident individuals who . . .	Responsible citizens who . . .
• have the essential learning skills of literacy, numeracy and information and communication technology • are creative, resourceful and able to identify and solve problems • have enquiring minds and think for themselves to process information, reason, question and evaluate • communicate well in a range of ways • understand how they learn and learn from their mistakes • are able to learn independently and with others • know about big ideas and events that shape our world • enjoy learning and are motivated to achieve the best they can now and in the future.	• have a sense of self-worth and personal identity • relate well to others and form good relationships • are self-aware and deal well with their emotions • have secure values and beliefs and have principles to distinguish right from wrong • become increasingly independent, are able to take the initiative and organise themselves • make healthy lifestyle choices • are physically competent and confident • take managed risks and stay safe • recognise their talents and have ambitions • are willing to try new things and make the most of opportunities • are open to the excitement and inspiration offered by the natural world and human achievements.	• are well prepared for life and work • are enterprising • are able to work cooperatively with others • respect others and act with integrity • understand their own and others' cultures and traditions, within the context of British heritage, and have a strong sense of their own place in the world • appreciate the benefits of diversity • challenge injustice, are committed to human rights and strive to live peaceably with others • sustain and improve the environment, locally and globally • take account of the needs of present and future generations in the choices they make • can change things for the better.

Figure 3.3 Revised aims for secondary school curriculum in England.

The Welsh Assembly Government's approach to education and lifelong learning is set in the broader context of our vision for children and young people overall.

We have seven core aims for children and young people developed from the United Nations Convention on the Rights of the Child. These will underpin all of the activities of DCELLS.

We aim to ensure that all children and young people:

- Have a flying start in life and the best possible basis for their future growth and development
- Have access to a comprehensive range of education, training and learning opportunities, including acquisition of essential personal and social skills
- Enjoy the best possible physical and mental, social and emotional health, including freedom from abuse, victimisation and exploitation
- Have access to play, leisure, sporting and cultural activites
- Are listened to, treated with respect, and are able to have their race and cultural identity recognised
- Have a safe home and a community that supports physical and emotional wellbeing
- Are not disadvantaged by any type of poverty.

The Learning Country 2: Delivering the Promise

Figure 3.4 The seven core aims for education in Wales (see Department for Children, Education, Lifelong Learning and Skills, 2008).

consultations, which raises the question about the extent to which democratic consultation contributed to the aims, as opposed to *policy borrowing* from different countries (Ball, 1994). But while the development and refinement of curriculum aims clearly shows evidence of policy borrowing there are significant nuances in the use of language. For example, Scotland and England's specification requires pupils 'to become . . .', which perhaps seeks to 'engineer' social characteristics, whereas the Northern Ireland aim to 'empower' young people to make informed and responsible decisions throughout their lives may be reflective of a more developmental approach. In Wales the aims signal a strong commitment to the development of young people's rights, but as ever the key question is to what extent this rhetoric results in teaching and learning that genuinely builds on children's rights. As we have shown, national curriculum aims have increasingly become more clearly specified and more detailed. However, of key interest are the ways in which aims become realised in the detail of programmes of learning (for in-depth exploration of this see John White's work, e.g. White, 2004). There are many facets to this, including organisation of subjects and/or areas of learning; the ways that programmes of learning are structured; the extent to which learning activities are specified; and the balance between different kinds of learning such as knowledge, skills, ways of thinking, etc. (see Chapter 6, this volume).

Many of the issues that emerge as a result of our comparison of national curriculum aims can be related to debates about priorities for educational systems more generally. One particularly important strand of debate historically has been about the nature of knowledge and the curriculum.

Key questions for reflection

Which elements of the national curriculum aims/aims for education in the four countries do you prefer, and why?

Knowledge and the curriculum

National curricula are built on particular conceptions of knowledge, and views about how people learn. A view of knowledge which has influenced the content-driven approach to curriculum construction in England is the idea of intrinsically worthwhile knowledge articulated by Matthew Arnold (1822–88) who was a poet, social commentator and former schools' inspector. While visiting schools as an inspector, Arnold became conscious of the inequalities of the English education system. In 1869 in a series of essays entitled 'Culture and Anarchy' Arnold made the case for the replacement of religious schools by a public education system in which all children would have access to a canon of knowledge drawing on 'the best that has been thought and said' (Arnold, 1869, p. viii). The subjects Arnold listed as the basis of a general liberal education included English, Latin, modern languages, history, arithmetic geometry, geography and nature study. David Conway claims that Arnold was the first person to suggest a national curriculum and that his thinking influenced not only the Education Act of 1870 but also the 1904 Regulations and a number of subsequent committees (Conway, 2010).

In the mid-1960s Peters argued the case for education as 'initiation into intrinsically worthwhile activities' taught in a way that evokes interest (Stenhouse, 1975, p. 9). He stressed the particular values to be derived from intellectual engagement with specific types of academic and theoretical learning (associated primarily with history, literature and the sciences). A decade later, Hirst declared that distinct disciplines or forms of sub-divisible knowledge (such as mathematics, physical sciences, human sciences, history, religion, literature and the fine arts, philosophy) constitute unique ways of understanding experience (Hirst, 1974, p. 46). Each has its own intrinsic logic, distinct concepts, distinct ways of determining truth and complex ways of understanding experience. Although Hirst stressed the purity of these forms of knowledge, he was at pains to point out that this did not automatically imply that the school curriculum should necessarily be constructed around discrete subjects.

As we have seen, however, the first national curricula for primary schools were strongly subject-based (although slightly less so in Scotland). The result was undoubtedly a 'preparatory style' curriculum (see Chapter 2) designed literally as preparation for later schooling. Such schooling also included the basics, where required, but with a greater emphasis on the full range of humanities and sciences, providing a route towards engagement with western European 'high' culture.

The development of a content-heavy national curriculum in England, and its influence on other countries, is considered to be both a response to and a reaction against the pressures of globalisation (Priestley, 2002; Goodson, 2005). On the one hand governments are seen to be responding to global market competition by trying, through educational policy making, to make countries more competitive. On the other hand governments are also considered to be reacting against perceived threats to national sovereignty.

Key questions for reflection

What are the important aspects of knowledge and how should these be represented in the primary curriculum?

Objectives-driven curricula

Objectives-driven curricula are based on pre-specified content and objectives accompanied by expectations that pupils' learning behaviours can be modified, and that the learning should be verified by observation and testing. This represents a classic rationalist view of curricula. Two of the most influential texts in relation to objectives-driven curricula in the modern era are those by Tyler (1949) and Bloom (1956). Tyler's book *Basic Principles of Curriculum and Instruction* was written to address what he considered to be four fundamental questions which must be answered in developing any curriculum and plan of instruction:

1.   What educational purposes should school seek to attain?
2.   What educational experience can be provided that are likely to attain these purposes?

3.   How can these educational experiences be effectively organized?
4.   How can we determine whether these purposes are being attained?

(Tyler, 1949, p. 1)

Tyler's argument in favour of objectives-led teaching was informed by his view that 'Many educational programs do not have clearly defined purposes. In some cases one may ask a teacher of science, of English, of social studies or some other subject what objectives are being aimed at and get no satisfactory reply' (1949, p. 3). His answer to his own questions was to argue that the curriculum should be set out in the form of fairly broad educational objectives and learning experiences that would inform the organisation of instruction, and the subsequent evaluation of outcomes. The assumption was that most student outcomes should be capable of being pre-defined and measured, and 'any statements of objectives . . . should be a statement of changes to take place in the students' (1949, p. 44). The idea of altering pupils' behaviour in ways seen to be beneficial by the education system is at the heart of Tyler's theory. However, he acknowledged that objectives were a matter of choice by schools, and that the selection or elimination of educational objectives should be informed by 'a comprehensive philosophy of education' (p. 4), for example, the development of democratic values, including 'opportunity for wide participation in society' (p. 34). In view of the example of democratic values that Tyler offers it is striking that his theory does not seek to take account of the voices of students themselves in establishing aims for their education (except in the sense that students' needs should be 'diagnosed' by teachers as one possible way to select objectives).

Building explicitly on Tyler's work, Bloom's committee of college and university examiners proposed a *Taxonomy of Educational Objectives* (Bloom, 1956) as a basis for 'a classification of educational outcomes' (p. 10). The taxonomy consists of six hierarchically organised elements: knowledge; comprehension (meaning understanding generally rather than the more limited notion of reading comprehension); application; analysis; synthesis (putting together parts and elements to form a whole); and evaluation. One of the key problems with the taxonomy is that its ultimate detail is revealed through test items (perhaps not surprising in view of the background of the committee who devised the taxonomy). Thus only those aspects that were amenable to testing were included in the taxonomy. (The distorting influence on the curriculum of inappropriate assessment is now much better understood although it is still a problem that bedevils modern curricula – see Chapter 5, this volume).

In the last ten years, as we illustrated in our example at the beginning of the chapter, it has become more and more common to see lesson objectives (or learning intentions) written onto the teacher's board and explicitly discussed as part of the lesson. Pupils are also encouraged to write the objectives into their books. As part of the same trend trainee teachers have been required to ensure that their lesson plans have short-term lesson objectives. But it is important to explore why an objectives-led approach has gained such prominence as a preferred way to structure teaching.

Primary teaching in England was significantly affected by the national literacy and numeracy strategies from 1997 to 2010. One particularly dominant influence was the need to plan literacy and numeracy teaching based on the lists of teaching objectives specified in the *frameworks for teaching*. These frameworks specified a series of lesson objectives laid out in termly blocks covering the primary school years (age 5 to 11). However, rather than explicitly refer to previous work, such as Tyler or Bloom, the model was based on more recent school-effectiveness research that had come to influence policy makers prior to the implementation of the strategies.

In a research paper that questioned the evidence base for the national literacy strategy framework for teaching Wyse (2003) challenged the model of teaching. An Office for Standards in Education (Ofsted) overview of school effectiveness research (Sammons *et al.*, 1995) had been cited as the support for the objectives approach. But when the cited evidence was examined, it became clear that the research evidence told a rather different story. One of the better publications cited in the Ofsted review pointed out that the links between appropriate instructional behaviour and the teacher's objectives had rarely been studied directly; instead an 'assumption' was made about objectives based on opportunity to learn data (Brophy and Good, 1986). Brophy and Good (1986) also observed that objectives vary in their nature and that this necessitates a range of teaching approaches such as: problem solving; decision making; essay composition; preparation of research reports; or construction of some product. In other words the evidence showed that some effective lessons may well be tightly focused around a short-term and clearly formulated lesson objective. Other lessons will be more effective if there is an overall goal, such as the publication of a class book, presentation or drama performance, which guides the teaching and learning. This process can lead to a range of valuable learning outcomes, which do not need to be pre-specified because they will depend on the pupils' response to the task and to the teachers' interaction with them.

Some 20 years later, in a large-scale research study of school reform in Arizona, Thomas Good (who had worked with Brophy in 1986) found that it was important to provide students with 'more opportunities for meaningful and appropriate task negotiation within their assignments, if not actual choices about what they study and how they learn it' (Good and McCaslin, 2008, p. 2489). Clearly if pupils make choices about their learning then it is not possible or appropriate for the teacher to pre-specify lesson objectives. This has the added advantage of freeing the teacher to plan learning experiences for pupils that build on their assessments of pupils and consideration of pupils' interests and motivation. Significant research evidence, therefore, questions the idea that most teaching should be structured around pre-specified lesson objectives, which in turn begs the question, why has this approach been pushed so hard by policy makers? There is no straightforward answer to this question. One reason is perhaps that the objectives approach is on the surface straightforward to understand, easy to communicate in media 'sound bites', and sounds like common sense. Whatever the reasons, advocacy for or against an objectives-driven approach is emblematic of a very long history of debate about the nature of the curriculum and its deeper aims and purposes.

The apparent simplicity of the objectives-driven approach masks a number of tensions relating to the nature of objectives, for example, the potential of inappropriately emphasising some and neglecting others; the associated danger of emphasising trivial rather than significant aspects of learning; the potentially limiting effect of pre-specified intentions; the associated danger of de-skilling teachers; the difficulty of predicting outcomes; and the neglect of unanticipated but potentially important outcomes (Smith

1996, 2000). Over time the trend towards micro-managing learning by breaking objectives down into smaller and increasingly mechanistic elements resulted in Tyler's 'generalist' intentions becoming distorted. Scott (2008) aptly summarises the continued, if unacknowledged, influence within contemporary curricula of the objectives focused and behaviourist goals, and the emergence of what he describes as a technicist, linear, atomised, pre-specified 'input-output' model of curriculum and assessment (Scott, 2008, pp. 25–30). His critique focuses on the unethical nature of a means-ends approach which seeks to turn teachers into technicians governed by pre-set goals and efficiency and effectiveness targets that take no account of the way pupils learn (Scott, 2008). Given that there is a weak theoretical and empirical justification to the objective model which has been so forcefully employed it is difficult not to see this as a means of control over pupils, teachers and educationists exercised by politicians and policy makers.

If the objectives-driven model is open to question as the main influence on the organisation of the curriculum and its aims, then there is a need to consider alternative philosophies. The process-driven, developmental approach to curriculum (also outlined in Chapter 2) envisages education as an interactive process of inquiry and values-clarification. The basis of this more child-centred and developmental approach to learning draws upon the diverse work of a wide range of theorists who focused variously on issues such as the nature of the curriculum; the centrality of the learner; the cognitive processes involved in learning; and the role of the teacher in the learning process. Pinar and colleagues characterise this as a paradigm shift away from preoccupation with institutionalised curriculum development (as exemplified by Tyler's rationale) towards an understanding curriculum through critical inquiry and practice (Pinar 2007).

Key questions for reflection

What are the advantages and disadvantages of objectives-driven curricula?

Why do you think politicians are attracted to objectives-driven curricula?

Why do you think the focus of curriculum studies has shifted towards better understanding practice?

Conclusions

We have shown in this chapter the many similarities and the significant differences between the aims for national curricula in the four nations. The countries of the UK engaged in different levels of consultation over different timescales in relation to elements of their national curricula. Scotland, Northern Ireland and Wales all seemed to have engaged in lengthy periods of consultation and incremental development of their new curricula. England latterly took this approach to the development of its secondary curricula but its primary curriculum has been bedevilled by a top-down approach where policy makers have decided on national curricula and only offered limited timescales for minimal consultation. It remains to be seen how successful the development of the

primary curriculum in England will be. Because national curriculum aims are so fundamental to the whole curriculum it is our view that particular care has to be taken to
establish aims, with exhaustive attempts made to reach consensus. But, as we have shown,
the policy borrowing trend has the potential to compromise democratic consultation.

Even when aims are satisfactorily consulted on, the development of the curriculum to
address the aims can result in undesirable consequences. For example, pressures to establish
canons of particular knowledge and 'great works' can distort more egalitarian aims.
Rationalist models of education have been and continue to be influential, even if proponents
are not able to explicitly articulate such distinctions. Even early objectives-driven models
that recognised that establishing curricula should be a matter of choice for schools (although
not pupils) have been corrupted to support countries' drives on *standards*. There is overall
a need for greater simplicity and precision in the wording of aims so that their impact
throughout the whole curriculum including, if appropriate, through subjects is genuine.
There is no point in having worthy aims if they are not realised in practice.

The most striking difference between the countries' approach is that taken by Wales to
locate their broad aims for education within the framework of the UN CRC. This is a
powerful signal that children's rights are deemed to be important. It is surely appropriate
that in the twenty-first century pupils' rights should be a central feature of any national
curriculum, not least because the countries who are signatories to the CRC (which all
four nations are) have a legal and moral obligation to fulfil their promises.

The main purpose of a school curriculum is to support children and young people's
learning and development. In our view this means that pupils themselves should have a
direct influence on the nature of the curriculum. This can be achieved in a variety of ways.
One way, as we have discussed, is to locate the curriculum in a children's rights framework. Another way is to make strenuous efforts to directly engage pupils in the development of new curricula, including its aims, and to pay attention to work on children's
voices. The curriculum itself, once it has been developed, also needs to offer genuine
choice to pupils over their curricula in a variety of ways including over the activities that
they undertake in their lessons and the directions these might take.

If pupil ownership were a central feature of the curriculum we would argue that the
following aims should inform national curricula:

- To engender passion for learning.
- To develop understanding of how human activity impacts on the sustainability of the
  planet and inculcate an active contribution to enhancing sustainability.
- To encourage choices over learning.
- To develop a critical understanding of power and how it is manifested in a range of
  societal contexts.
- To understand how to collaborate with others to achieve better outcomes for all
  concerned.
- To prepare for a 'good life'.

To varying degrees aspects of these are evident in the national curricula of the four
nations, but no curriculum currently has a child-centred curriculum informed by all these
aims.

At the time of writing this book the Conservative–Liberal Democrat coalition government in England had set aside both the Cambridge Primary Review and the Rose recommendations and instigated yet another review of the national curriculum for primary schools. One of the terms of the review was to 'give teachers greater professional freedom over how they organise and teach the curriculum' (online, 2011). However, a parallel remit of the review was to specify a core curriculum based on international comparison with 'highest performing jurisdictions'. This raises questions about how the balance of control between nationally and locally determined curricula can be resolved. It also says very little about pupils' rights to the curriculum. The challenge offered by White (2004) remains relevant, that government's prime responsibility is for a well-worked-out set of aims.

Teacher education/training task

Investigate the extent to which the national curriculum aims of one country relate to the national curriculum programmes of study.

Further reading

1. Dewey, J. (1902). *The Child and the Curriculum*. Chicago: University of Chicago Press.
   The classic account of the curriculum from one of the most influential educational thinkers. Short, readable and still relevant.
2. White, J. (2010). Aims as Policy in English Primary Education. In R. Alexander, C. Doddington, J. Gray, L. Hargreaves and R. Kershner (eds), *The Cambridge Primary Review Research Surveys*. London: Routledge, pp. 282–305.
   An important contribution which informed independent advice on the revision of the primary curriculum in England in 2008 which has been largely ignored by government.
3. Kelly, A.V. (2009). *The Curriculum. Theory and Practice* (6th edition). London: Sage.
   A comprehensive outline of approaches to curriculum construction highlighting the importance of values and beliefs within practice.

References

Arnold, Matthew (1869). *Culture and Anarchy: An Essay in Political and Social Criticism*. Oxford: Project Gutenberg.

Ball, S. (1994). *Education Reform: A Critical and Post-structural Approach*. Buckingham: Open University Press.

Bloom, B.S. (ed.). (1956). *Taxonomy of Educational Objectives. Book 1 Cognitive Domain*. New York: Longman/David McKay Company, Inc.

Brophy, J. and Good, T. (1986). Teacher Behaviour and Student Achievement. In M.C. Wittrock (ed.), *Handbook of Research on Teaching*. New York: Macmillan, pp. 328–375.

Cambridge Primary Review (2008). Introducing the Cambridge Primary Review, available from www.primaryreview.org.uk.

Conway, D. (2010). *Liberal Education and the National Curriculum*. London: Civitas, Institute for the Study of Civil Society.

Council for the Curriculum Examinations and Assessment (CCEA) (2007). *The Northern Ireland Curriculum Primary*. Belfast: CCEA.

Cunningham, P. (2011) *Politics and the Primary Teacher*. London: Routledge.

Department for Children, Education, Lifelong Learning and Skills (2008). *Framework for Children's Learning for 3 to 7-year-olds in Wales.* Cardiff: Welsh Assembly Government.

Dunne, J. (1993). *Back to the Rough Ground. Practical Judgement and the Lure of Technique.* Notre Dame, IN: University of Notre Dame Press.

Good, T. and McCaslin, M. (2008). What We Learned about Research on School Reform: Considerations for Practice and Policy. *Teachers College Record*, 110(11), 2475–2495.

Goodson, I. (2005). The Crisis of Curriculum Change Taboo Issue 1, available from www.ivor-goodson.com/s-CrisisofCurriculum-1.

Harland, J., Moor, H., Kinder, K. and Ashworth, M. (2002). Is the Curriculum Working? The Key Stage 3 Phase of the Northern Ireland Curriculum Cohort Study. Slough: NFER.

Hirst, P. (1974). *Knowledge and the Curriculum: A Collection of Philosophical Papers.* London: Routledge and Kegan Paul.

House of Commons Children, Schools and Families Committee (2009). *National Curriculum. Fourth Report of Session 2008–09. Volume 1.* London: House of Commons.

Kelly, A.V. (2009). *The Curriculum: Theory and Practice* (6th edition). London: Sage.

Le Métais, J. (1997). Values and Aims in Curriculum and Assessment Frameworks. (Original INCA hyperlink to this document no longer live but document available through Google search).

Pinar, W.F. (2007). *Intellectual Advancement Through Disciplinarity: Verticality and Horizontality in Curriculum Studies.* Rotterdam: Sense Publishers.

Priestley, Mark (2002). Global Discourses and National Reconstruction: The Impact of Globalization on Curriculum Policy. *Curriculum Journal*, 13(1), 121–138,

Qualifications and Curriculum Development Authority (QCDA) (2009). National Curriculum. Retrieved 26 August 2009, from http://curriculum.qca.org.uk/index.aspx.

Ross, A. (2000). *Curriculum Construction and Critique.* London: Routledge.

Sammons, P., Hillman, J. and Mortimore, P. (1995). *Key Characteristics of Effective Schools: A Review of School Effectiveness Research.* London: Office for Standards in Education (OfSTED) and Institute of Education University of London.

Scott, D. (2008). *Critical Essays on Major Curriculum Theorists.* London: Routledge.

Scottish Government (2011). Curriculum for Excellence, available from www.ltscotland.org.uk.

Smith, M.K. (1996, 2000). Curriculum Theory and Practice. *The Encyclopaedia of Informal Education,* available from www.infed.org/biblio/b-curric.htm.

Stenhouse, L. (1975). *An Introduction to Curriculum Research and Development.* London: Heinemann.

Tyler, R. (1949). *Basic Principles of Curriculum and Instruction.* Chicago: University of Chicago Press.

White, J. (ed.) (2004). *Rethinking the School Curriculum: Values, Aims and Purposes.* London: RoutledgeFalmer.

Wyse, D. (2003). The National Literacy Strategy: A Critical Review of Empirical Evidence. *British Educational Research Journal*, 29(6), 903–916.

Chapter 4

Pedagogy

Vivienne Marie Baumfield

Chapter summary

The chapter begins with an examination of the concept of pedagogy, which is a term that is still unfamiliar in the British context. The first section considers its meaning, the relationship between the teacher and the learner that it describes and the implications for our understanding of teachers' identity and professionalism. In the second section of the chapter, the characteristics of teaching and learning in the primary school classroom are discussed and an overview is given of changes in policy that have had an impact on pedagogy. This section also refers to some of the major research projects that have studied primary classroom practice since the Plowden Report and considers the challenge for the teacher who needs to balance competing demands for learner-centred and subject-based teaching. Finally, the potential offered by a focus on learning processes through interventions such as Thinking Skills, Learning to Learn and Assessment for Learning to support teachers in adopting an 'inquiry stance' and taking control of their pedagogical practice is evaluated.

What is pedagogy?

In *The Child and the Curriculum* (Dewey, 1990), the role of the teacher is described as building a bridge between the world of the child and the intellectual, cultural life of the community, a task that requires a deep understanding of both the logical structure of subject knowledge and of the learner's psychological development. For the child, informal learning outside the classroom is a continuous, integrated process with no conscious division between experience, inquiry and knowledge; a process in which interest is assured and relevance can be taken for granted. However, the range of such experience may be idiosyncratic and it is through formal education that children can participate in the wider cultural and social life of the community. Understanding and maintaining the balance between the interest of the learner and the requirements of the subject to be studied makes great demands on the teacher, who faces the challenge of achieving the same integration when learning in school settings as would occur naturally outside the classroom. Pedagogy articulates the complexity of teaching, highlighting the need for teachers to make well-informed choices in their selection of the strategies they use to build a bridge between the learner and the curriculum. Pedagogy is a term that is not used very much in the UK where the dynamic relationship between teaching, learning and culture it signifies is underplayed in restricted definitions of teaching as simply instruction (Simon, 1981). The difference between teaching and pedagogy is one of scope as teaching describes the actions taken whilst pedagogy focuses not only on the actions but also the ideas and values of education that need to be considered. Encompassing the interactions through which knowledge is shared between generations through formal education, pedagogy is both the art and science of knowing how to conduct intentional and systematic intervention in order to influence the development of the learner. If we have only a limited understanding of what teaching and learning involves, we diminish the professionalism of teachers. We also fail to recognise that teaching is an activity with the potential to preserve or subvert cultural values and so can never be neutral (Nyborg, 1993; Olson and Bruner, 1996).

In Ancient Rome the 'paedagogus' was an educated slave, often a Greek, engaged in the schooling of the children of the elite. The term literally means to lead a child to school and the modern usage of pedagogy retains this sense of the teacher as both the guide and the servant of the learner. It is the task of the teacher to educate rather than coerce or merely entertain the students in their charge. The concern of all teachers is to create experiences that provide encouragement for students to learn something that is meaningful to them in the here and now and an interest in continuing to learn in the future. Authentic pedagogy is achieved when the teacher is willing to make their intentions explicit, is able to demonstrate coherence between theories held about learning and their practice, and is open to challenge from different perspectives, including those of the learners themselves, on the effective mediation of learning. Commitment to authentic pedagogy puts the emphasis on developing professional judgment rather than on trying to achieve total mastery of subject content:

> In most cases, the teacher cannot in the nature of the case be an expert. It follows that he [*sic*] must cast himself in the role of a learner. Pedagogically this may in fact be a preferable role to that of the expert. It implies teaching by discovery or inquiry methods rather than by instruction.
>
> (Stenhouse, 1975: 91)

It is not only unrealistic to expect teachers, particularly primary teachers, to have total command of a subject, it also shows a lack of understanding of what it is that teachers do need to know. The danger in focusing too much on mastery of content is that curriculum 'subjects' become manufactured, simplified, agreed versions of a complex field of knowledge with little relationship to the world outside the school. The expertise of the teacher lies in the ability to understand how a particular subject is constructed, what it means to think like a scientist or a historian, and therefore how to structure teaching so that someone else can learn. Dewey referred to this process as 'psychologizing the subject' so that the requirements of learning are made explicit to the learner. Emphasis on the processes of learning rather than on the content does not mean that teachers do not need to know anything about the topic they are teaching but does recognise that what is important is being able to model what it means to learn. As a teacher you should be confident enough to admit when you don't know something and able to show the children how to find and evaluate information. Teachers who think of themselves as pedagogues rather than instructors have more command over the way in which they approach learning and teaching and can make better use of their rich, contextual knowledge of the learners in their classrooms. Such teachers are willing to take on more responsibility as they cannot simply rely on delivering a curriculum devised by someone else and need to be 'autonomous professionals' who continue to develop their knowledge, understanding and skills through the systematic interrogation of their practice in the classroom (Stenhouse, 1975).

Pedagogy encompasses the means by which the teacher takes hold of the 'moments of contingency' (Black and Wiliam, 2009), the teachable moments, as they occur in the classroom. It has an immediacy requiring observation and judgment so that decisions can be made as events occur in the fast-moving interactions between the teacher and the learner and between learners (Banks *et al.*, 2005). The values and beliefs of the teacher and the role of education in society influence these decisions and inform the judgments made. Thinking about teaching in this way emphasises the skills of the teacher who must successfully negotiate between the rock and the hard place formed by context, content, child and learning in the complexity of real classrooms (Gipps and MacGilchrist, 1999: 55). Understanding this process puts teacher professionalism at the heart of school improvement because how successful schools are ultimately depends on what teachers do and think, 'It's as simple and as complex as that' (Fullan and Hargreaves, 1991: 117).

Questions for reflection

Do you agree with the statement that teachers need not have complete mastery of subject content? How much should a teacher know about a topic they are teaching?

Primary school classrooms

The distinctive feature of the progressive movement that led up to and culminated in the Plowden Report (DfE, 1967) was the perspective of teachers on the nature of children's learning. One of the most memorable phrases in relation to the work of primary teachers was, 'We teach children not subjects', which is reflected in the emphasis, particularly in the infant classroom, on the individual child's development, a belief that learning through play is important and the preservation of the child's natural curiosity (Pollard, 1994). One of the most persuasive advocates of this approach in the classroom is Sybil Marshall who in her book, *An Experiment in Education*, describes her experiences as a teacher in a one-room school in rural Cambridgeshire:

> I had been struggling to impart some knowledge of contour lines, without much success . . . The trouble was that we lived in such a flat country that it was really very

difficult to relate the lines on the map to the actual countryside. Somehow I had to demonstrate the meaning of all the curious squiggles on our maps. We had a hundredweight of potter's clay in an old bin outside . . . we used it to create an island. We pinned white paper carefully to a table and then emptied the clay-bin bit by bit on to the paper, moulding the wet, sticky clay into hills and valleys and cliffs and beaches and promontories . . . (and learning all these geographical terms as we went along) . . . Then with a mighty concerted effort, we heaved the whole island up just far enough for someone to pull out the paper from beneath it . . . The paper showed very clearly the outline of the island at sea level: for the first time many children understood an outline map properly. We then made a wire cutter, exactly like a grocer's cheese cutter . . . and proceeded to cut off layers of our clay island. Each time we cut it, we placed the lump we had cut off on to the original outline map and drew round it. When we had finished we had a complete contour map of our island which everyone understood . . . Then we played other games with it. We created storms by raining on the island with a watering can . . . we watched where the water ran between the hills and marked out the course of the rivers . . . Now rivers and peaks began to be claimed by the children, and when at last one of the more romantically minded boys invented a cove full of buried treasure, geography gave way to English and story writing . . . (when the) clay became too dry, cracked and crumbled (it) disappeared back into the bin from which it came. By that time, no doubt, somebody had led us away to something new, though I cannot now remember what it was.

(Marshall, 1963: 56–57)

In this extract the need for spontaneity and the freedom to follow the interest of the child is presented eloquently and a convincing case is made for the value of the 'integrated day', where subjects are explored through themes. However, there is also recognition of the need to understand substantive concepts such as contour lines related to the curriculum for geography, which was the impetus for this particular 'experiment' in education. Elsewhere in her book, Sybil Marshall discusses the need to balance the competing demands of fostering creativity and enabling children to acquire basic skills.

Even at the height of the trend in primary education for child-centred learning it was not as prevalent in classrooms as was often supposed. Two major studies of classroom practice in primary schools, Primary Assessment Curriculum Experience (PACE) and the Observational and Classroom Learning Evaluation (ORACLE) both found little evidence of the supposedly prevalent 'laissez-faire' discovery learning approach practised by teachers acting as peripatetic advisers rather than teaching 'properly' reported in the popular press. In reality, even when teachers held strong views on the importance of child-centred learning, there was a gap between beliefs and practice as they faced the practical dilemmas of managing limited resources and dealing with large classes. In the PACE project (Pollard, 1994) the dynamic affecting pedagogy in the primary classroom prior to the National Curriculum is represented as the negotiation of the tension between successfully 'balancing' the competing demands of child-centred approaches and basic skills at one end of the spectrum or the 'coping' strategies employed at the other end of the spectrum in order to meet the demands of simply getting through the school day.

The greater the degree of overt political interference in this delicate balancing act, the more difficult the teacher's task can become, as a teacher explained:

> The problem with being a primary teacher now is that there is no consensus about what we do. Parents, teachers and educationalists all want something different. There is a pressure from people outside to get back to the '3 Rs' with a centralized curriculum. Everything I aspire to is creative, informal, child-centred; but what I worry about is making sure the children acquire the basic skills. I want to marry those two approaches – but I think I'll always feel pulled in those opposite directions.
>
> (Pollard, 1994: 150–151)

This teacher was one of the respondents in a major study looking at the impact of the Education Reform Act (DfE, 1988) on life in primary school classrooms. Whilst I will argue that the pressures identified here have become more acute since 1988, the fundamental dilemma between the responsibility to nurture the whole child and the necessity of inculcating the basic skills as the foundation for subsequent learning is an enduring one. In Chapter 2, we saw that whether schools should be regarded as elementary schools, preparatory schools or progressive, developmental schools has been a concern since the inception of state-funded primary education. The introduction of the Education Reform Act was itself a response to a particularly acrimonious turn in this debate triggered by events in one inner London school. Conflict among the staff of William Tyndale School between those advocating a radical child-centred approach, in which the children were given the freedom to choose what and how to learn, and those who believed that children would be disadvantaged if they were not first schooled in basic literacy and numeracy, became a national issue. As is often the case with public debate about education, fact was obscured by rhetoric and what was in essence an issue concerning the local management of schools in London became the focus for a national campaign to get 'back to basics' in the curriculum (Davis, 2002).

The ORACLE project was a large-scale five-year observational study of primary classrooms in England which started in 1976, in the aftermath of the William Tyndale School controversy with the aim of 'mak(ing) a modest contribution to the debate on primary education which should now be carried out in a more conciliatory and informed manner, with less conviction on either side that they hold a monopoly of truth' (Galton et al., 1980: xvi). In 1996, there was a follow-up study looking at the situation in the primary school classroom in the same schools 20 years later (Galton et al., 1999). The team found that in many respects there had been little change over the years. The physical layout of the classroom remained the same with children still sitting around tables in mixed groups working on individual tasks. Writing and listening to the teacher still dominated most lessons and the level of cognitive demand remained low, learning to solve problems, for example, was not any more noticeable as a feature of lessons than before. Closer examination of patterns of activity in the classrooms '20 years on' did reveal some changes, both positive and negative, with significant implications for pedagogy and teacher professionalism. One beneficial aspect of the changes that had occurred was that, despite an increase in direct instruction at the expense of more active learning approaches, pupils were not only talking to each other more, they were more likely to be talking about the work rather than being engaged in social chat. Consequently, whilst the impact of the emphasis on 'whole class instruction' from the work of the School Improvement movement (Mujis and Reynolds, 2005) meant that group work remained the least used strategy in the primary classroom; when it did occur, it was more purposeful. However, the introduction of the subject-based National Curriculum in 1988 had a subtle but profound impact on the interactions between teachers and their pupils in the primary classroom, which was detrimental. Primary schools began to have a subject timetable similar to that of a secondary school and this put pressure on the time available in the school day. The biggest difference pre- and post-1988 was in the time that teachers had to observe and monitor pupils in informal ways as part of the normal business of teaching.

In England direct intervention into pedagogy, as opposed to indirect influence through curriculum reform, came into effect for the first time through the introduction of the National Literacy Strategy (NLS) and the National Numeracy Strategy (NNS) (DfEE, 1998, 1999). The strategies were introduced in response to the concerns of policy makers regarding the attainment of pupils in international comparative studies and built upon the research into school improvement by researchers who advocated interactive, whole-class teaching as the most effective approach to improving literacy and numeracy in primary schools (Muijs and Reynolds, 2005). It was at this time that we find the term 'pedagogy' being used for the first time in policy documents by the Head of the Teacher Training Agency (now Teacher Development Agency). Unfortunately, the scope of the term is reduced so that it becomes a synonym for 'teaching methods' and the concept turned on its head so that rather than empowering teachers as professionals, autonomy is reduced as it is deemed that the selection of methods should not be 'at the whim of individual teachers to determine in their classrooms' (Alexander, 2001: 542). In the NLS Framework for Teaching, successful teaching was described as 'discursive, characterised by high quality oral work' and 'interactive, encouraging, expecting and extending pupils' contributions' (DfEE, 1998: 8). Similarly, the NNS Framework states: 'high-quality direct teaching is oral, interactive and lively . . . in which pupils are expected to play an active part by answering questions, contributing points to discussion, and explaining and demonstrating their methods to the class' (DfEE, 1999: 11). In both strategies, the emphasis is on an interactive model encouraging a two-way process of interaction between the teacher and the pupils. However, when the impact of the strategies on actual classroom practice was investigated, it was found that:

> new 'top-down' curriculum initiatives like the NLS and NNS, while bringing about a scenario of change in curriculum design, often leave deeper levels of pedagogy untouched. Traditional patterns of whole class interaction persist, with teacher questioning only rarely being used to assist pupils to articulate more complete or elaborated ideas as recommended by the strategies. The findings also raise questions about the effectiveness of the in-service training programmes which have accompanied the national strategies.
>
> (Smith *et al.*, 2004: 409)

This reveals tension in the idea of pedagogy as an important element of teacher autonomy. Whilst some might see the positive aspect of the fact that classroom practice can be impervious to authoritarian intervention from policy makers, the persistence of styles of interaction known to be less effective in promoting learning remains a source of concern. The solution to this apparent intransigence of practice in the face of research evidence can be found and has been demonstrated through the promotion of teacher professional development based on an 'inquiry stance' (Cochran-Smith and Lytle, 2009), as we shall see in the final section of this chapter.

Whilst the introduction of the literacy and numeracy strategies may not have shifted ingrained patterns of interaction it did put further strain on teachers in the management of the time available in an already overcrowded curriculum. This reduction in time combined with the increased demands for recording and reporting pupil progress imposed by inspection, particularly in England and Wales, resulted in increased workloads and little space in which to respond to individual children. The delicate balancing act that enabled teachers to practice the art of teaching by applying pedagogical principles in a responsive, flexible manner (Gage, 1985) was jeopardised by these external demands.

Questions for reflection

How much freedom should an individual teacher have in determining how they approach learning and teaching in their classroom? What would be an appropriate balance between autonomy and accountability to outside agencies in professional practice?

Finding room for manoeuvre: support for the development of pedagogy in the primary classroom

It may appear to be stating the obvious to say that teachers' views on how children learn influence how they approach teaching in their classrooms but it took a long time for research to be done that explored the nature of the link between theories of learning and pedagogical practices in any depth (Bennett, 1988). Early work in this area focused on identifying 'teaching styles' and attempted to link these with pupil attainment but it quickly became apparent that there was no simple or direct correlation. Intensive study of 26 teachers of children in their last year of primary school in England (Gipps and MacGilchrist, 1999) found that although teaching repertoire is related to views of how children learn, the views held by each individual teacher are complex and do not offer clear support for any one theory of learning. Learners' views of learning also influence what teachers do and studies have identified a tension felt by primary school children between a desire for the enjoyment that can come from exercising independence with a degree of risk and a fear of failure. As the child progresses through primary school, anxiety can increase so that 'playing safe' by pleasing the teacher tends to become dominant (Pollard, 1990, 1994). Of course, the learner's perception of what the teacher wants may well be at odds with what the teacher actually intends and is often the source of a tendency towards conservatism in classroom practice. Black and Wiliam (1998) have studied the process whereby classroom contracts are negotiated between teachers and students and highlight how the opening moves in such negotiations, on both sides, will be determined by epistemological, psychological and pedagogical beliefs. The actual or perceived implications of external pressures can, as we have seen, also distort what happens in classrooms. Gipps and MacGilchrist (1999) found that although not one of the teachers in their study believed that children learn solely from the transmission of facts, a quarter of them felt pushed into doing more of this because of the amount of work to be covered by the National Curriculum and the requirements of testing. They conclude that although finding room for manoeuvre in such challenging situations is complex, it is not impossible:

> Teachers need to be able to understand the multi-dimensional nature of pedagogy, they need to exhibit the characteristics of effective learners if they are to continue to improve their own pedagogy so as to maximise their impact on the learning of the pupils they teach.
>
> (Gipps and MacGilchrist, 1999: 47)

As we have seen, the importance for teachers to be learners themselves was stressed by Dewey in his recommendations for teacher education at the beginning of the twentieth century and subsequently promoted by Lawrence Stenhouse in his advocacy of teachers as researchers. The ideal of the teacher as a research engaged professional conducting systematic inquiry into their practice is enduring but has proved difficult to realise. However, interventions such as Thinking Skills (Baumfield, 2006), Learning to Learn (Higgins *et al.*, 2007; James, 2007) and Assessment for Learning (Black and Wiliam, 1998) led by teachers in partnership with researchers have had some success in enabling teachers to develop the diagnostic skills and willingness to engage in continuous professional learning. It is interesting that it was at a time when the capacity for teachers to participate in curriculum development, believed by Stenhouse to be the most fruitful area in which to work towards developing an 'inquiry stance', was severely restricted that these developments took place. It is as if the focus on learning processes that is characteristic of these approaches acted as a surrogate for the engagement in curriculum development that teachers had lost when the National Curriculum was imposed in England, Wales and Northern Ireland and a more prescriptive approach was adopted in Scotland. Not everyone welcomed these developments and there was a division within the policy community between those who supported teacher inquiry as a means of finding out 'what works' and those, such as Chris Woodhead, the Chief Inspector of Schools, who ridiculed what he termed the 'lunacy of learnacy' (Woodhead 2002).

A systematic review of research into the impact of thinking skills approaches on teachers found that a common thread running through all the studies was shift in teachers' attention so that they focus more on the learning process (Baumfield, 2006). They are able to learn more from their students and describe the classroom as a positive environment where they are able to respond and develop their practice to facilitate greater student responsibility and autonomy. The importance of a teacher being a learner in the classroom is stressed and in one study they talk of the teachers developing greater empathy with their students. What appears to be particularly powerful is the combination of positive reinforcement for teachers from the enthusiastic response of their students combined with a degree of cognitive dissonance as their perceptions of the capabilities of their students are subverted. Dissonance itself is not necessarily a novelty for teachers who may frequently experience the unexpected in the complex world of the classroom. However, the surprises are usually disconcerting and unwelcome and much energy goes into reducing complexity and any scope for subversion in the arduous transition form novice to expert practitioner (Brown and McIntyre, 1993). The value of thinking skills approaches in the classroom is that they have characteristics that engage and motivate learners whilst supporting teachers in effecting a pedagogy that promotes social constructivism in an open-ended but structured, and therefore manageable, environment. As learners articulate and discuss their ideas the teacher gains new insight into the thinking of their pupils. It is this positive dissonance and the subsequent adjustment of perceptions and expectations that stimulate teacher inquiry and is the basis for growth. What the systematic review found to be true of thinking skills can also be seen in reports of the impact of Learning to Learn and Assessment for Learning as they share the key features of employing powerful pedagogical strategies to promote mutual, reciprocal and cumulative classroom dialogue. It is such dialogic teaching that is promoted in the Cambridge Primary Review as the key to developing 'a pedagogy of repertoire rather than recipe, and of principle rather than prescription' (Hofkins and Northern, 2009: 28). The following description of a lesson in a primary school where the teacher was using a thinking skills approach illustrates how a simple tool such as an 'odd-one-out' exercise (Baumfield and Higgins, 2001) serves as a powerful pedagogical strategy for the promotion of dialogic teaching.

'You can agree with people when they are not your friend and you don't even like them.' I overheard this comment whilst listening to a group of infant school children discussing a thinking skills activity in their 'Healthy Eating' lesson. They were doing an 'Odd-one-Out' exercise looking at three images of food and their task was to work in groups to decide which was the odd one out and give a reason. The teacher displayed the images on the 'Big Book' stand at the front of the class and the children worked in pairs to decide which food item was different from the other two and were told to be ready to give a reason for their choice. The teacher then invited the pairs to tell the class about their choice and this generated many different options each with a supporting reason that justified the choice. The activity develops skills in categorising and classifying information as well as encouraging reasoning. As well as the cognitive skills promoted through the activity, the teacher gains valuable insight into the prior knowledge of pupils and can identify any misconceptions. Like many thinking skills activities, it is a valuable tool for diagnostic and formative assessment. Thinking skills activities also promote the disposition to enquire and to be reasonable through the emphasis on paired and group work in solving problems.

In the infant school class I observed, the plenary focused on how best to decide between the different choices by evaluating them in terms of the objective of the lesson, which was to identify 'healthy' and 'unhealthy' foods. The discussion was lively as all the groups had made different decisions and had equally strong reasons to support them. The discussion would not have been out of place in a sixth form philosophy lesson as the merits of deciding how many factors could support a view as opposed to weighting factors according to their importance – quality versus quantity – were reviewed. This emphasis on the promotion of a disposition to value the opinion of others, to evaluate arguments using explicit criteria and to exercise good judgment is at the heart of thinking skills approaches.

Questions for reflection

One teacher described the moment of surprise when listening to student feedback as the 'Wow' factor as it made her think, 'Wow! I've never thought about it like that'. Can you identify any instances when a student has made you think differently about something you have been teaching them? Did the surprise stimulate your own learning? Did it change the way you teach?

Recommendations

The situation across the four nations of the UK (with the possible exception of England where the direction of reform remains uncertain) is currently one of change as curriculum reform shifts the focus from the prescription of content and outcomes towards seeking to understand the experiences and processes that support learning. The implications of these changes for the role and identity of the teacher is once again focusing attention on the requirement to be an autonomous, research-engaged professional. Engaging in inquiry requires teachers to access strategic and reflective thinking in order to consider the meaning of their activity in holistic as well as analytic ways:

> This kind of thinking is important when embarking on activities which make considerable demands on a person, such as an academic or vocational course or project. It can also be extremely valuable in dealing with . . . a challenge to an assumption, belief or a communication problem. Most significantly, it is what changes what could be a routine process into a learning experience.
>
> (Moseley *et al.*, 2005: 315)

If we are to build on what we already know about how to support such professionalism, the initial education and continuing professional development of teachers needs to have some key features:

- An orientation towards teaching as a process of lifelong learning through inquiry.
- Access to powerful pedagogical strategies to support student learning through promoting fruitful classroom dialogue that supports diagnostic feedback and provide tools for teacher inquiry.
- Promotion of schools as learning communities in which teachers can learn from each other and share best practice.
- Closer integration of theory and practice through partnership between schools and universities in the identification and investigation of pedagogical issues.

We know that initiatives incorporating these features can be designed and implemented successfully but if they are to be sustained, they need to form part of policy. We can find some grounds for optimism regarding the professional development of teachers in recent reviews of teacher education in Scotland and Wales where there is evidence of a willingness within the policy community to consider radical rethinking of the nature of teacher professionalism. The process of curriculum reform can support teacher agency and provide room for the development of the research-engaged professional but the impact of the economic recession on the provision of initial and continuing teacher education is a threat.

Conclusion

The task of building the bridge between the child and the curriculum is central to pedagogy and so the challenge of achieving a balance between the ideals of child-centred learning and the requirement to equip the learner with the basic skills endures. The challenge increases when there is a reluctance to consider pedagogy as essentially complex and teaching is simply seen as a technical activity. The ability of primary school teachers to move beyond coping strategies and achieve a balance is compromised further when the curriculum is overloaded with content and when assessment is externally imposed and focused on accountability rather than supporting learning.

One of the major changes over recent years has been the gradual contraction of 'informal' time in classrooms and the consequent reduction in spontaneity, responsiveness to the child's interests and opportunities for conversations with individual children about their work. Teachers are, however, resourceful and room for manoeuvre was found through initiatives such as Thinking Skills, Learning to Learn and Assessment for Learning, which provided scope for dialogic teaching and teacher inquiry. However, not all teachers benefited from such initiatives and there is still a need to embed the concept of the research-engaged professional teacher in the policy and practice of initial and continuing teacher education.

Teacher education/training task

1.   Look at the different guidelines and regulations for the registration of teachers in the UK[1] and compare what they say about the role and responsibilities of the teacher. Make a note of any explicit references to the following:
     • pedagogy
     • inquiry
     • research.
2.   Discuss how your own education as a teacher has equipped you for the task of 'leading the learner into learning'.
3.   If pedagogy connects the act of teaching with the wider society, what is the role of the community in the education of children in schools?

Recommended reading

Alexander, R.J. (2001) *Culture and Pedagogy: International Comparisons in Primary Education*. Oxford and Boston: Blackwell.

Robin Alexander is one of the leading researchers on pedagogy and this book provides an introduction to the fundamental concepts and also provides a conmparative perspective which serves to highlight the particularities of the UK context. He also makes the connections between inquiry, classroom dialogue and pedagogy in current research that are discussed in this chapter.

Dewey, J. (1990) *The School and Society and the Child and the Curriculum*. Chicago: University of Chicago Press.

This new edition of the book first written in 1902 provides one of the best introductions to the central dilemmas of the role of the teacher. I have used his idea of building a bridge between the child and the curriculum in this chapter and this book provides further insight into the complexity of the teacher's role in the classroom.

Marshall, S. (1963) *An Experiment in Education*. Cambridge: Cambridge University Press.

I discovered this book whilst working on this chapter and wished that I had known about it when I was training to be a teacher many years ago. It is a window into an age that has passed but it remains relevant to today because of the insight it gives into the role of the teacher and for the opportunities for discussion it provides. Sybil Marshall is inspirational in her passion for teaching and her honest account of the challenges she faced and the creative solutions she found remains stimulating.

Note

1   www.tda.gov.uk/training-provider/itt/qts-standards-itt-requirements.aspx?sc_lang=en-GB; www.gtcs.org.uk/standards/standard-initial-teacher-education.aspx; www.deni.gov.uk/index/ teachers_pg/teachers-teachinginnorthernireland_pg.htm; http://teachertrainingcymru.org/ node/23.

References

Alexander, R.J. (2001) *Culture and Pedagogy: International Comparisons in Primary Education*. Oxford and Boston: Blackwell.

Banks, F., J. Leach and B. Moon (2005) Extract from 'New Understandings of Teachers' Pedagogic Knowledge'. *The Curriculum Journal* 16 (3): 331–340.

Baumfield, V.M. (2006) Tools for Pedagogical Inquiry: The Impact of Teaching Thinking Skills on Teachers. *Oxford Review of Education* 32 (2): 185–196.

Baumfield, V.M. and S.E. Higgins (2001) *Thinking Through Primary Teaching*. Cambridge: Chris Kington.

Bennett, N. (1988) The Effective Primary School Teacher: The Search for a Theory of Pedagogy. *Teaching and Teacher Education* 4 (1): 19–30.

Black, P. and D. Wiliam (1998) Assessment and Classroom Learning. *Assessment in Education* 5 (1): 7–73.

Black, P. and D. Wiliam (2009) Developing the Theory of Formative Assessment. *Educational Assessment, Evaluation and Accountability* 21: 5–13.

Brown, S. and D. McIntyre (1993) *Making Sense of Teaching*. Buckingham: Open University Press.

Cochran-Smith, M. and J. Lytle (2009) *Inquiry as Stance: Practitioner Research in the Next Generation*. New York: Teachers College Press.

Davis, J. (2002) The Inner London Education Authority and the WIlliam Tyndale Junior School Affair, 1974–1976. *Oxford Review of Education* 28 (2/3): 275–298.

Dewey, J. (1990) *The School and Society and The Child and the Curriculum.* Chicago: University of Chicago Press.

DfE (1967) Children and their Primary Schools (Plowden Report). London: HMSO.

DfE (1988) Education Reform Act. London: HMSO.

DfEE (1998) National Literacy Strategy. London: HMSO.

DfEE (1999) National Numeracy Strategy. London: HMSO.

Fullan, M. and A. Hargreaves (1991) *What's Worth Fighting for? Working Together for Your School.* Andover, MA: Regional Laboratory for the Educational Improvement of NE and Islands.

Gage, N.L. (1985) *Hard Gains in the Soft Sciences: The Case of Pedagogy.* Bloomington, IN: Phi Delta Kappa.

Galton, M., B. Simon and P. Croll (1980) *Inside the Primary Classroom.* London: Routledge and Kegan Paul.

Galton, M., L. Hargreaves, C. Comber, T. Pell and D. Wall (1999) *Inside the Primary Classroom: 20 Years On.* London: Routledge.

Gipps, C. and B. MacGilchrist (1999) Primary School Learners. In P. Mortimore (ed.) *Understanding Pedagogy and its Impact on Learning.* London: SAGE, pp. 46–67.

Higgins, S., K. Wall, V.M. Baumfield, E. Hall, D. Leat, D. Moseley and P. Woolner (2007) *Learning to Learn in Schools Phase 3 Evaluation Year Three Final Report.* London: Campaign for Learning.

Hofkins, D. and S. Northern (eds) (2009) *Introducing the Cambridge Primary Review.* Cambridge: Cambridge Primary Review.

James, M. (2007) *Learning How to Learn: Classrooms, Schools, Networks.* London: Taylor & Francis.

Marshall, S. (1963) *An Experiment in Education.* Cambridge: Cambridge University Press.

Moseley, D., V.M. Baumfield, S.E. Higgins, J. Elliott, M. Gregson, D. Newton and S. Robson (2005) *Frameworks for Thinking.* Cambridge: Cambridge University Press.

Muijs, D. and D. Reynolds (2005) *Effective Teaching: Evidence and Practice.* London: SAGE.

Nyborg, N. (1993) *Pedagogy.* Haugesund: Nordisk Undervisningsforlag.

Olson, D.R. and J.S. Bruner (1996) Folk Psychology and Folk Pedagogy. In D.R. Olson and N. Torrance (eds) *The Handbook of Education and Human Development: New Models of Learning, Teaching and Schooling.* Oxford: Blackwell, pp. 9–27.

Pollard, A. (1990) *Learning in Primary Schools: An Introduction for Parents, Governors and Teachers.* London: Cassell.

Pollard, A. (1994) *Changing English Primary Schools? The Impact of the Education Reform Act on Key Stage 1.* London: Cassell.

Simon, B. (1981) Why No Pedagogy in England? In B. Simon and W. Taylor, *Education in the Eighties.* London: Batsford, pp. 125–145.

Smith, F., F. Hardman, K. Wall and M. Mroz (2004) Interactive Whole Class Teaching in the National Literacy and Numeracy Strategies. *British Educational Research Journal* 30 (3): 395–411.

Stenhouse, L. (1975) *An Introduction to Curriculum Research and Development.* London: Heinemann.

Woodhead, C. (2003) *Class War: The State of British Education.* London: Little Brown.

Chapter 5

Has anyone really learned anything?

Assessment in the primary school

Louise Hayward

Chapter summary

Assessment has received a very bad press over the last 20 years. This has mainly been because of the high stakes testing of statutory tests and targets. However, there are signs of interesting new developments including those that build on the formative processes of Assessment for Learning. The chapter presents a new diagram that illustrates the ways that learners are at the centre of assessment which is closely linked to curriculum and pedagogy. The final section of the chapter looks at the different ways that the four nations have approached statutory assessment, and reveals some surprising variation.

Introduction

What did you think when you read the word assessment in the title of this chapter? The word assessment often brings with it fairly negative and slightly fearsome connotations. It may remind people of unpleasant or stressful experiences they have had with assessment, for example an important test or examination or the feeling caused by a less than entirely positive comment about learning made by a teacher. We all have assessment memories and the power of these memories tells us how much assessment really matters. In this chapter we will take a step back to rethink what assessment is all about in primary schools and how it relates to curriculum and to pedagogy. Rather than seeing assessment as something rather intimidating to be kept at bay, we will begin to explore how assessment can be used to bring the curriculum to life, to enhance children and young people's experiences in learning and to provide essential evidence for teachers to support them in their quest to enhance learning. We will also reflect, briefly, on wider uses of assessment information and explore the challenges we all face as we strive to keep a strong focus on what matters, on learning.

Few areas of education are more contentious than assessment. Newspaper headlines abound telling of falling standards and failing schools but fewer headlines tell of the quiet revolution that has been under way. Internationally, assessment is being transformed from something to be feared to a force for good, integrating curriculum and pedagogy in ways that promote better life chances for every learner. This chapter is the story of that transformation. In this book earlier chapters have dealt with the importance of the curriculum as the means by which society determines what it believes to matter in the learning conversation across generations. Earlier chapters have also dealt with the importance of pedagogy, the approaches to learning and teaching most likely to lead to deep, meaningful learning and confident, motivated learners. As the third corner of the learning triangle assessment is the process by which we gather information to help teachers and learners discern if anyone has actually learned anything. The chapter explores how assessment can be used to support learning as it is taking place and to discern over time what learning has taken place. Summarising progress in learning should reflect on both how much learning has taken place and how well that learning has been undertaken.

The learning triangle presented in Figure 5.1 illustrates the relationship between curriculum, pedagogy and assessment. There are two important things to note. The first is that learners and learning are at the heart of the process. If curriculum defines what is to be learned and pedagogy describes how learning takes place then the role of assessment is to gather evidence to support leaning and to allow all to discern the extent to which learning is taking place. However, although policy documents in England, Northern Ireland, Scotland and Wales each profess to support this position, the translation of these ideas into practice is complicated in large part by the number of uses made of assessment information. Although the main aim of assessment should always be linked to learning, assessment can and often is used in a myriad of ways, for example to inform decisions about how successful teachers or schools are in improving children's learning – or to provide information on examination results to parents as a means of helping them to choose a school for their child. Without much difficulty, Paul Newton identified 22 uses of assessment information (Newton, 2007). When assessment is used for too many purposes the learning triangle can be turned on its head with assessment at the top driving what is taught within the curriculum and how it is taught. For example, if the stakes are high and teachers believe that they will be judged by the test results of the children in their class or if headteachers believe that their school will be judged by their test results, then teachers will teach to the tests. If tests were to represent all that mattered in the curriculum then having them dominate teaching and learning might not be a problem. However, all too often tests only measure limited areas of the curriculum. These limited areas then become the focus of most of the activity in classrooms and the original intentions of the curriculum become distorted. In addition, high stakes tests can also lead to less desirable pedagogies. There is a great deal of evidence that when the assessment

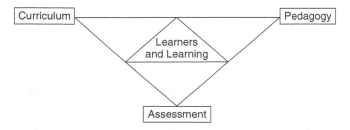

Figure 5.1 The learning triangle.

stakes are high approaches to teaching and learning change. In his book, *Testing Times: The Uses and Abuses of Testing* (2008), Gordon Stobart takes a balanced view of the impact of the high stakes assessment culture in England arguing that 'there have been benefits in England from these pressures'. For example, he argues that accountability testing indicates that 'improvement is expected' (p.122). However, in the chapter entitled 'The long shadow of accountability' Stobart provides an extensive evidence base describing how internationally testing has had a significant impact – not always a positive one – on curriculum and pedagogy.

Key questions for reflection

Think about two of your own powerful assessment memories, one positive and one less positive.

Make a list of why you would describe the first memory as positive.

Make a separate list of why the second memory was less positive.

Compare the two lists and thinks about what made the difference.

What might be the implications from your own experiences for the way that you work with learners?

Assessment – a principled stance

Like many other areas of education, assessment has its own language and, again in common with many areas of education, assessment language causes problems. Often people use terms such as 'formative assessment' and 'summative assessment' as if they refer to different *kinds* of assessment. Thus, formative assessment is sometimes taken to mean the assessment approaches that teachers use as part of their day-to-day activities and summative assessment is associated mainly with tests. This can be confusing: for example, if information from a test is used to inform learning, then is the assessment formative or summative? To avoid such confusion in this chapter we use the terms 'formative' and 'summative' to refer to the *purposes* of the assessment. Thus, if the teacher's main purpose is to support a child's or children's learning then the assessment has a formative purpose; evidence is being used in the formation of the child's learning. Black and Wiliam (2009: 9) argued that

> Practice in a classroom is formative to the extent that evidence about student achievement is elicited, interpreted, and used by teachers, learners, or their peers, to make decisions about the next steps in instruction that are likely to be better, or better founded, than the decisions they would have taken in the absence of the evidence that was elicited.

This is *Assessment for Learning.*

If the teacher's main purpose is to sum up what the child or children has/have learned – for example, to give information to another teacher, to a parent or carer, to another school or to government – then the purpose is summative. This is *Assessment of Learning*. It is information from Assessment of Learning that is all too often expected to serve a wider range of purposes leading to the distortions in curriculum and pedagogy discussed earlier in this chapter.

In recent years considerable attention internationally has been paid to exploring how assessment might be developed in ways that will enhance learning. In 2002, the Assessment Reform Group (a group of internationally recognised assessment researchers who have sought to bring research, policy and practice in assessment into closer alignment) proposed a definition for Assessment for Learning. They argued that

> Assessment for Learning is the process of seeking and interpreting evidence for use by learners and their teachers to decide where the learners are in their learning, where they need to go and how best to get there.

In order that this might happen, the group proposed ten principles:

Assessment for learning
- Is part of effective planning;
- Focuses on how students learn;
- Is central to classroom practice;
- Is a key professional skill;
- Is sensitive and constructive;
- Fosters motivation;
- Promotes understanding of goals and criteria;
- Helps learners know how to improve;
- Develops the capacity for self-assessment;
- Recognizes all educational achievement.

(ARG, 2002)

A number of important points to note arise from these principles.

Assessment as part of curriculum

The first point is that assessment as part of learning is built in from the first stages of thinking about the curriculum and about teaching and learning. It is part of effective planning. As teachers begin to think about what it is that they intend children should learn they also pay attention to what kinds of evidence they might collect to help discern the extent to which children's learning is consistent with or challenges their expectations. Planning should also pay attention to the creation of tasks that are sufficiently open to allow learners to demonstrate learning which is not needlessly limited by the nature of the task. Thus, assessment should allow all educational achievement across the curriculum to be recognised, not only the learning initially identified by the teacher.

The interaction of assessment and pedagogy

A second key point relates to pedagogy, in particular the relationship between teacher and learner. The principles focus on learning and emphasise the importance of learners' understanding the goals and criteria – what they are learning, why that learning matters and what evidence they might look for when reflecting on what progress they have made in their own learning. The principles emphasise the importance of learners themselves actively taking part in that process and themselves assessing progress. The principles also identify understanding and practising Assessment for Learning as key to what it is to be a professional teacher, working with learners to build their confidence and their commitment.

Assessment to inform future learning

Third, the principles suggest that assessment is future focused. Rather than concentrating on assessment as evidence of past learning, the concern is with assessment as an evidence base from which to build future learning. The feedback shared with learners should point both to what future progress might be made and to how such progress might best be achieved.

These principles may appear to focus on subtle changes to existing classroom practices but despite their gentle exterior, they are radical. Marshall and Drummond (2006) differentiate between the letter and the spirit of Assessment for Learning. In the next section of this chapter we will deal with these ideas in greater detail but the key issue to note here is that it is important to understand that Assessment for Learning involves putting into practice the principles described earlier in this chapter. These principles represent the *spirit* of Assessment for Learning. Often, however, Assessment for Learning is described as a *set of classroom techniques,* for example traffic lights, wait time. If techniques are not linked to a deep understanding of what it is that they are trying to achieve then they may represent the letter of Assessment for Learning but not the spirit; as such, they are unlikely to have the beneficial effect on learning that is the central purpose of Assessment for Learning.

Since the establishment of the Assessment Reform Group's assessment principles all four countries of the UK have engaged in significant efforts to introduce Assessment for Learning into their schools. In England, although there have been several attempts to introduce this kind of assessment, the dominance of the high stakes testing environment has been evident. Despite the fact that much of the original work on Assessment for Learning was developed in England in the King's College Medway Oxford Assessment project by Paul Black and colleagues (Black *et al.*, 2003), the ideas emerging have been more wholeheartedly taken up with varying degrees of success by the education systems in the other three parts of the UK. Scotland established the Assessment is for Learning programme in 2001, Northern Ireland the Assessment for Learning project in 2004, and Wales the Developing Thinking and Assessment for Learning programme in 2005.

In each of the four countries in the UK, numbers of teachers in primary classrooms were involved in developing classroom cultures true to the spirit of Assessment for Learning. Building from research evidence on what matters in the creation of more engaged, successful learners, they developed a range of approaches to put ideas into practice. The individual strategies described in this section are the results of some of these teachers putting principles into practice. It was crucial to link clearly the *idea* of what mattered for learning with the *strategy* to put this idea into practice in the classroom. However, in some cases, as greater numbers of teachers were introduced to ideas of Assessment for Learning this link all too often became lost. In such cases the introduction focused only on the techniques, which when used without rationale or understanding have little chance of making the positive difference to learning first claimed for Assessment for Learning in the original Black and Wiliam research review (1998).

Involving pupils in the process of identifying what is to be learned is an important way to engage and to motivate learners. Teachers have found different ways of doing this. For example, one primary teacher, one week before she began the class topic on farming with her ten-year-old pupils, put up a large empty poster on the wall of her classroom and asked the pupils to make notes on the poster of the kinds of things that they would like to learn about farming. She also contributed to the collection of ideas. On the first day of the topic she then discussed and collated these aims with the class and together they agreed a plan for the project. The teacher reported that the levels of engagement and the quality of topic work from the class had been significantly better than she had expected.

This kind of activity is very different from the more common 'sharing' of learning aims, where the teacher simply makes the learning aims explicit, for example, by putting them on the classroom wall. In this context although the word 'sharing' is used what is actually happening is closer to telling. Being involved in deciding what they want to learn is an important factor in motivating learners. Motivation matters and, as one primary pupil suggested,

> if we do what we want to do, then we'll learn it better but if it is all the teacher's idea, then maybe we'll say, hmmm . . .

Another teacher was concerned that in her class only a small number of children appeared to be engaging in discussion. She suggested:

> It's always the same children who put up their hands and although I try to involve the others it really doesn't work. The children who don't put their hands up seem unhappy when I ask them to answer and the children who have their hands up feel frustrated that I don't ask them!

To help address this issue she changed the way discussions were organised in her classroom. She discussed the issue with the children and agreed with them that in future no one would put up their hand in classroom discussion. Different approaches would be used in different circumstances. For example, it was agreed that when big (or open) questions were asked each person would first be given time to think for themselves and then would have an opportunity to discuss their thoughts with others. The class would then discuss what a good response to the original questions would be like. From this discussion criteria were identified that groups would use to decide on the quality of presentations. Each group would then together agree on their response and present their ideas to the class who could ask questions and offer comments using the criteria as the framework for their feedback. In this way more people in class were more actively involved in the process and the teacher was able to use evidence from the presentations to explore how the children's thinking was developing.

Points for reflection

Reflect on the examples of practice on classrooms offered in the previous section of this chapter. Identify a way in which you might support learners to become more actively engaged in your classroom.

Think about a classroom you have been working in recently. What kinds of assessment were going on and what were their purposes?

Think about something that you plan to teach. Reflect on what is important in your teaching plan and develop approaches to assessment that will ensure that you gather evidence on what matters. Share your ideas with a colleague and consider the extent to which the information you will gather reflects what you have identified as being important in the curriculum.

Assessment for Learning – a community endeavour

Recognising the complexity of the emerging relationship between research, policy and practice in Assessment for Learning, an international group of assessment researchers reviewed previous attempts to define Assessment for Learning. At the Third International Conference on Assessment for Learning (2009) held in Dunedin, New Zealand, they redefined Assessment for Learning.

> Assessment for Learning is part of everyday practice by students, teachers and peers that seeks, reflects upon and responds to information from dialogue, demonstration and observation in ways that enhance ongoing learning.

This group believed that this new definition was necessary because of the difficulties that they had witnessed across the world in the various attempts made to put assessment principles into practice. In a position paper developed following the conference (Dunedin, 2009: 1) the group argued that:

> the ways in which the words are interpreted and made manifest in educational policy and practice often reveal misunderstanding of the principles, and distortion of the practices, that the original ideals sought to promote. Some of these misunderstandings and challenges derive from residual ambiguity in the definitions. Others have stemmed from a desire to be seen to be embracing the concept – but in reality implementing a set of practices that are mechanical or superficial without the teacher's,

and, most importantly, the students', active engagement with learning as the focal point.

In an attempt to avoid misinterpretation, the group expanded on key ideas in their redefinition of Assessment for Learning. This process of letting readers inside the heads of those who had thought through the new definition of Assessment for Learning is consistent with ideas being advocated by the group to teachers as they work with learners.

The Dunedin group suggested that 'everyday practice' should be seen as the 'interactive, dialogic, contingent relationships of teaching and learning' (2009: 2). The researchers imply in this statement that learning conversations (among learners and between teachers and learners) must have at their centre negotiation of the relationship between learning and teaching. These conversations must include opportunities for sharing thinking amongst learners and teachers, for building on current understandings and for seeking to clarify misunderstandings in order to make progress in learning. These kinds of conversation, not yet common practice in many schools and classrooms, have to be built into the day-to-day practices of teachers and learners if assessment is really to support learning.

Second, the group highlighted the order in which they placed 'students, teachers and peers'. Students were listed first to emphasise that it is they who are at the heart of the learning process. This idea is not new and terms such as 'student centred learning' have become so common that it is almost possible to read them without thinking what they really mean (see Sue Rogers' forthcoming book in this series for an up-to-date analysis of child-centred education). Everything in teaching should be focused on student learning. The purpose of teaching is not to get through the curriculum and to allow teachers to feel that they have worked hard. The essence of all educational activity in all schools is learning. However, despite their best intentions teachers cannot learn for students. The intention behind all that a teacher does in planning for learning, in designing good tasks, in sharing criteria, in encouraging rich questioning and in providing feedback should be to encourage learners to become autonomous. Ultimately the teacher's activities should serve as models for learners to develop such skills for themselves.

Third, the Dunedin group commented on the importance of the phrase, 'seeks, reflects upon and responds to'. They argued that this phrase highlighted the importance of Assessment for Learning as a process of enquiry. This process involves teachers and learners actively seeking evidence of what learners are able to do and what they understand and using that evidence to help identify appropriate next steps in learning.

A number of implications for teachers emerge from this set of ideas. The first relates to the seemingly simple idea of 'next steps'. If teachers are to offer support in helping learners towards worthwhile next steps in learning, they have to have a good understanding of what progression might look like within that particular area of the curriculum. They also need to have a sophisticated understanding of pedagogy and of how different approaches to learning might be used to support learning most effectively. It is the synthesis of these professional understandings combined with the careful collection of evidence related to individual learners or groups of learners that allows teachers and learners to support progression in learning. The second issue is that evidence about learning may point not only to next steps for learners but also to next steps for teachers. The evidence collected may, for example, suggest the need for changes to the teacher's planned curriculum or to the need for changes to the proposed pedagogy. Thus Assessment for Learning is also assessment for teachers' learning.

The final issue to which the Dunedin group drew attention related to the phrase, 'information from dialogue, demonstration and observation'. In discussion the group commented on the range of evidence that might be available to teachers. Evidence might be available from verbal communication, both oral and written, and from non-verbal behaviours. Further, they indicated that evidence can come from activities planned by teachers but also from unplanned events, for example, where a learner demonstrates knowledge, understanding or skill in an unexpected way. The teacher's planned curriculum should not restrict the learning that pupils are able to demonstrate. Much of the evidence about learning is likely to come from observation of day-to-day activities in schools and classrooms and from conversations between teachers and learners. Occasionally, teachers may decide to use a special task or test to collect evidence and, although the Dunedin group recognised that information from such tasks or tests can be used formatively, they describe them as 'not essential' and warn of the potential for those to become 'frequent mini-summative assessments'.

The Dunedin definition of Assessment for Learning sets it within socio-cultural theory. Hayward (2012) argues that Assessment for Learning is a vehicle for socio-cultural transformation in schools and classrooms. When Assessment for Learning is at the heart of practice in a classroom, learning will be far more of a community endeavour; this will be very different from the traditional classroom relationship between teacher and learners. For example, in a traditional primary class there might be one teacher and 30 learners; in an Assessment for Learning classroom there will be 31 learners. In this mutually respectful learning environment the teacher works with learners, sharing professional expertise and involving learners in all aspects of the learning process, from planning to discerning how much and how well progress has been made. The community beyond the school also plays a more significant role in learning. Rather than being expected to support the school in passive ways, for example, by attending parent/carer meetings, parents, carers and members of the community would become co-learners helping to make connections between school learning and the wider world of the child in her/his community. Hayward (2012: 126) argues that the most distinctive change in such classrooms would be that the 'the traditionally quiet voices of learners and parents (would) become louder and more influential'.

Key questions for reflection

How would you describe the difference between the 'spirit' and the 'letter' of Assessment for Learning?

Think about the Dunedin definition of Assessment for Learning.

> Imagine that you have just visited a classroom where you have been really impressed
> by the Assessment for Learning. Describe what made you come to that judgement.
> For example, what was going on in the classroom? You may also wish to think
> about roles and relationships.

Assessment of Learning

This chapter has intentionally focused in the main on Assessment for Learning for this is
the major purpose of assessment in the primary school. This final section will consider
Assessment of Learning, that is, the ways in which assessment information might be used
to sum up where children are in their learning to provide a snapshot for the children or
their teachers or parents. We will also explore the ways in which assessment information
can be used for wider purposes, for example to judge the quality of teaching, the quality
of schools or the quality of education nationally and internationally.

For time to time teachers, or teachers and learners, will want to use information from
assessment to reflect on where learners are in their progress. In the first section of this
chapter we discussed the relationship between curriculum, pedagogy and assessment and
the importance of making sure that assessment supports curriculum and pedagogy.
Therefore, when teachers think about summing up the progress of individual learners this
should relate to the curriculum, to what matters in learning. When assessment is valid (or
when it has validity) there is a close relationship between assessment and the curriculum,
that is, information on learning is available for all that was identified as important when
the curriculum was planned. This may sound obvious but it is not always easy to achieve.
For example, a topic plan may make reference to the importance of children
understanding the way that people lived in Victorian Britain. It may also make reference
to the importance of groups working together to research, analyse and present
information. If the assessment information used to judge progress focuses only on the
product of the topic (understanding life in Victorian Britain), then important information
may be missing on the children's research skills, on their strategies for analysis or on their
approaches to collaboration. If these are important ideas in the curriculum plan then it is
important that evidence is collected to discern progress.

In a research review carried out for the EPPI centre (Evidence for Policy and Practice
Information and Co-ordinating Centre) Harlen (2004) identified five actions by teachers
likely to improve the quality of their assessment for summative purposes.

First, the research evidence indicates that, at all stages and for all purposes, learners should
be helped to understand what matters in their work, that is, the criteria by which their work
will be assessed. The review suggests that the most effective way of doing this is to provide
and to discuss practical examples of what meeting the criteria would look like in practice.
These practical examples help learners make connections between words and ideas.

Second, the research evidence points up the value of teachers making explicit the
reasons why particular grades have been given. It is also important that decisions about
grades are made using the relevant explicit criteria and that other factors, for example
behaviour, are not part of the decision-making process unless identified as a criterion.

Third, when teachers discuss assessment with learners they should emphasise what they are expected to learn rather than having a focus on the grade. Focusing on getting a high grade encourages pupils to learn for the test rather than learn effectively and deeply.

Fourth, teachers should seek to develop an understanding of progression in curricular areas and reflect on the progress learners are making in that context rather than developing detailed checklists. Harlen suggests that this is important not only for pupils as learners but also for teachers as learners.

> In this way summative assessment helps teachers' understanding of learning goals as well as facilitating more detailed knowledge of their students.
>
> (Harlen, 2004: 8)

Finally, the research evidence suggests that teachers need opportunities to develop their skills and understanding if they are to become both competent and confident in Assessment of Learning. The evidence suggests that teachers need time to work together to discuss assessment and issues that arise from putting ideas into practice in their own classrooms. They also require opportunities to plan assessments together and to moderate their judgements of evidence of learners' progress.

When information from teachers' judgements of Assessment for Learning is to be used for wider purposes, for example, to inform parents/carers of progress or to pass information to another teacher or another school, then it is important that the information is reliable. That means that when looking at the same profile of pupil work different teachers would make similar judgements. In primary schools most decisions about Assessment of Learning are likely to be 'best fit'. That means that the judgements that teachers make are most likely to relate to pupil progress using a range of evidence including, for example, evidence from teachers' observations, from what pupils have said, from what they have written or from products they have made. This range of evidence may also include information from tests either designed by the teacher or designed externally. If teachers choose to use externally designed tests then it is important to recognise both their potential and their limitations (Stobart, 2008). Looking at the range of evidence available the teacher will make a 'best fit' judgement comparing the evidence to the description of the grade or level. This process, supported by opportunities for teachers to be actively involved in moderation activities, can provide good evidence to share with other teachers, schools or parents. These forms of teacher assessment have the advantage that teachers can collect information from across the curriculum and come to common agreement on the 'best fit' whilst recognising that assessment always involves an element of approximation.

National governments in the four countries of the UK have in recent years held different views of the relationship between teacher summative assessment and externally designed tests in primary schools. In England there has been a strong commitment to the value of externally designed tests to drive up attainment. The balance has been different in other parts of the UK where there has been a stronger emphasis on developing teachers' Assessment of Learning practices. However, the importance of having an appropriate infrastructure on which to build Assessment of Learning practices was recognised at an international research seminar held at the University of Oxford in 2011.

Daugherty (2011) argues that although often there was a policy commitment to teacher based Assessment of Learning, the infrastructure to support that process was missing; without the appropriate infrastructure questions would remain about the quality of teachers' judgements in Assessment of Learning.

In the opening section of this chapter, the problem of trying to use assessment information for multiple purposes was introduced. Education, on the whole, is funded by public money and so politicians have a right to ask questions about its quality, for example, how well an education system is serving the needs of society or how good are its schools. Different governments have taken different approaches in trying to raise the quality of educational opportunities for children in primary schools. In England, for example, tests have been used to judge how well a school is performing and action is taken as a consequence of the test results. At the time of writing (2011) all children take National Curriculum Tests towards the end of Key Stage Two (at the end of primary school) in literacy, numeracy and science. Test results for schools are published and, therefore, the stakes are high for individual schools.

In Northern Ireland children in primary schools undertake computer-based adaptive tests (InCas) that focus on the progress made by individual pupils. These tests are 'adaptive' in that they respond to the pupil; initially, questions are based on the pupil's age but subsequent questions are selected depending on the pupil's response to the initial questions. The intention is that pupils are not presented with too many questions that are either too easy or too difficult for them. The evidence from these tests is used to inform a pupil profile which is shared with parents. Traditionally Northern Ireland has used information from national transfer tests to determine which children should gain access to grammar schools. It is intended that InCas replace the primary secondary transfer test. However, problems have been widely reported in the press about inaccurate results being made available to parents and the system has some way to go to gain the public credibility necessary for it to replace the high stakes transfer tests.

In Scotland, there are no compulsory tests in primary schools. Assessment information is based entirely on teachers' professional judgement. In addition, information on the educational system is made available to government through the Scottish Survey of Literacy and Numeracy, a sample survey that does not identify individual children or schools but samples performance in a range of schools across the country. Scotland also has a National Assessment Resource comprised of examples of curriculum, pedagogy and assessment designed and developed by teachers, available online for other teachers to consider on GLOW, a national intranet for all of Scotland's schools.

Wales no longer has national tests for children in primary schools. The system is similar to Scotland in that there is a strong emphasis on teachers' professional judgement. Wales has also invested significantly on processes of moderation.

For governments trying to discern how well their schools are performing, the task is complex. There is an ever increasing evidence base to suggest that too strong a focus on accountability and on competition amongst schools may not have the effect desired by politicians. Indeed, rather than closing the attainment gap, the gap between the performance of pupils who perform well in school and those who do not perform well, it may serve to widen the gap (Mons, 2009; Klenowski and Wyatt-Smith, 2011).

Table 5.1 PISA 2010 results across the UK

	Reading	*Maths*	*Science*
England	494 – joint 27th of 67	493 – joint 28th of 67	515 – 16th of 67
Northern Ireland	499 – joint 19th of 67	492 – 30th of 67	511 – joint 19th of 67
Scotland	500 – joint 15th of 67	499 – 21st of 67	514 – 17th of 67
Wales	476 – joint 38th of 67	472 – 40th of 67	496 – joint 30th of 67

The attraction of comparing the performance of one country's children against the children of other countries has become an increasingly influential element in education internationally. Perhaps the most famous of all of the international tests is PISA (Programme for International Student Assessment). Although this test is taken by pupils towards the end of their schooling, aged 15, the results of PISA often have implications for primary schools and teachers. The test is designed to explore the extent to which pupils have developed some of the knowledge and skills necessary to participate fully in society.

The 2010 PISA results are shown in Table 5.1.

The reaction, as reported on the BBC website, was that the then Welsh Education Secretary called the results 'unacceptable' and said everyone involved should be 'alarmed' (www.bbc.co.uk/news/uk-wales-11930257).

Statements such as this from government ministers often lead to action in both primary and secondary schools. However, a number of questions arise. To what extent is action justified? How reliable is a difference of 15 to 20 points on a scale with more than 500 points? What other evidence beyond this one test is available to inform the kinds of action necessary? To what extent does the action necessary relate to classroom practice rather than to the school system (e.g. qualifications system, selection)? To what extent does the action necessary relate to the school system rather than to the need for changes in other aspects of wider society, for example, health, housing, poverty of aspiration? The evidence from sources of assessment such as PISA may indeed require a nation to ask questions of itself but often the answers are sought in alternative forms of assessment, commonly more tests, and there is little evidence to suggest that this approach will address the issue identified. Action taken too quickly and based on insufficient evidence may be as bad as taking no action at all.

Conclusion

Assessment means nothing unless the focus is learning. In the first section of this chapter the focus was on how teachers might learn from assessment evidence to support learners more effectively. We highlighted the important role that learners must play in their own learning. We then reflected on different purposes of assessment, Assessment for Learning where the purposes are formative and Assessment of Learning where the purposes are summative. We argued that an understanding of the principles of assessment is a crucial part of having assessment work to support learning as the third corner of the learning triangle of curriculum, pedagogy and assessment. Finally, we reflected on how governments attempt to learn from assessment evidence and pointed to some of the dangers of basing too many decisions on a single source of evidence.

The title of this chapter asked a question – is anyone really learning anything? To be able to answer that question we need to be confident that in our society as a whole people become more assessment literate, that is, they understand more about assessment, what it can and cannot do and what makes it a powerful tool in supporting learning. Assessment Literacy is important for teachers and learners, for parents and politicians. As a society in the UK we may yet have some way to travel before we can be confident that the answer to the question is yes. Assessment research, assessment policy and assessment practice need to be brought into closer alignment. Perhaps reading this chapter is your own first step in building your own deeper understanding of assessment.

Key questions for reflection

Having read this chapter make a note of the main things that you remember.

Identify one or two actions that you intend to take in your own classroom and why you intend to take these actions.

How will you involve learners in this process?

How will you know if your actions are making a positive difference?

Share your ideas with a teaching colleague and learn together.

References

Assessment Reform Group (2002) *Assessment for Learning: 10 Principles*. Cambridge: University of Cambridge School of Education.

Black P. and Wiliam, D. (1998) 'Assessment and classroom learning', *Assessment in Education*, 5(1), 7–73.

Black, P. and Wiliam, D. (2009) 'Developing the theory of formative assessment', *Journal of Educational Assessment, Evaluation and Accountability*, 21, 5–31 .

Black, P., Harrison, C., Lee, C., Marshall, B. and Wiliam, D. (2003) *Assessment for Learning: Putting it into Practice*. Maidenhead: Open University Books.

Daugherty, R. (2011) Designing and implementing a teacher-based assessment system: Where is the infrastructure? Presented at the Oxford University Centre for Educational Assessment international seminar on Teachers' Judgments within Systems of Summative Assessment: Strategies for Enhancing Consistency, available at http://oucea.education.ox.ac.uk/wordpress/wp-content/uploads/2011/07/Daugherty-FINAL.pdf (last accessed 1 May 2012).

Dunedin Position Paper on Assessment for Learning from the Third International Conference on Assessment for Learning (2009), available at http://annedavies.com/PDF/11D_Position PaperAFL-NZ.pdf (last accessed 27 September 2011).

Harlen, W. (2004) A systematic review of the evidence of the impact on students, teachers and the curriculum of the process of using assessment by teachers for summative purposes. In

Research Evidence in Education Library. London: EPPI-Centre, Social Science Research Unit, Institute of Education, University of London, available at http://eppi.ioe.ac.uk/cms/Link Click.aspx?fileticket=OdG3t7IX5EY%3d&tabid=120&mid=942 (last accessed 1 May 2012).

Hayward, L. (2012) 'Assessment and learning: the learner's perspective', in John Gardner (ed.), *Assessment and Learning*, pp. 125–139, 2nd edn. London: Sage.

Klenowski, V. and Wyatt-Smith, C. (2011) 'Assessment for learning in the accountability era Queensland, Australia', *Studies in Educational Evaluation*, 37, 78–83.

Marshall, B. and Drummond, M.J. (2006) 'How teachers engage with Assessment for Learning: lessons from the classroom', *Research Papers in Education,* 21(2), 133–149.

Mons, N. (2009). 'Theoretical and real effects of standardized assessment'. Background paper to the study 'National Testing of Pupils in Europe Objectives, Organisation and Use of Results', EACEA; Eurydice, Belgium, available at http://eacea.ec.europa.eu/education/eurydice/documents/thematic_reports/111EN.pdf (last accessed 1 May 2012).

Newton, Paul E. (2007) 'Clarifying the purposes of educational assessment', *Assessment in Education: Principles, Policy & Practice*, 14(2), 149–170.

Stobart, G. (2008) *Testing Times: The Uses and Abuses of Assessment*. Abingdon: Routledge.

Chapter 6

Curriculum construction

Carmel Gallagher and David Egan

Chapter summary

The main influences on the structure of national curricula in the four nations are identified in this chapter. The links between the national curriculum of 1988 and policy in the four nations are addressed first. This section is followed by an account of the similarities and differences between the national curriculum construction in the four nations following devolution. The final section of the chapter considers the place of pedagogy in relation to the curriculum, and in particular the extent to which teachers have autonomous control over pedagogy and whether newly qualified teachers have the capacity to use this control.

The structure of the school curriculum in England, Wales, Northern Ireland, and to a lesser extent Scotland is the combined legacy of what was described in Chapter 2 as the 'nationalised curriculum' that emanated from the Educational Reform Act of 1988. Since 1999 the devolution of power from Westminster to national assemblies/parliaments in Belfast, Cardiff and Edinburgh, has allowed greater difference and distinctiveness to emerge across the UK. In considering the curricula which have emerged in the four nations since devolution, this chapter adopts a 'policy historiography approach' (Gale, 2001, p. 385) focusing on the substantive issues of policy, the nature of the curricula created and the place of professionals in this. Gale's concept of policy historiography aligns with the idea of contexts of text production (Bowe *et al.*, 1992; Ball, 1993, 1997) through which official policy, such as statutory curriculum documents, are produced.

Global educational reform from the 1980s onwards in rich and poor nations alike has been driven strongly by economic agendas. The prime motive appears to be to maximise the skill and qualification levels of populations as a way of enhancing competitive advantage in an increasingly global economy (Rizvi and Lingard, 2010; Leitch, 2006; Mckinsey and Company, 2009; OECD, 2010). This has led, in many countries, to an increased emphasis on national and international testing, greater school choice through marketisation and privatisation of services, and a focus on enhancing school effectiveness and accountability. This increasingly instrumentalist approach has led to a perception of the curriculum as something to be 'delivered' (Mundy, 2005; Fullan, 2010; Barber, 2007; Barber and Mourshed, 2007).

The emergence of this type of policy discourse in the UK in the late 1980s has been attributed in part to the predominance of neo-conservative elements within government exercised by 'a general sense of the nation-state being in economic decline and subject to globalization and to amalgamation in the wider European community' (Priestley, 2002, p. 133). Endorsing these views other commentators have pointed to the significant proportion of young people who leave full-time education with low or no qualifications. Low levels of educational participation and achievement, primarily associated with socio-economic disadvantage and low aspirations, has led many governments to reflect on the potential role of education in achieving greater social justice (Cassen and Kingdon, 2007; Goodman and Gregg, 2010; Gutman and Akerman, 2008).

Policy discourse of this nature has exerted strong influences on curriculum and assessment policies, leading to an increased emphasis both on the 'traditional academic' curriculum, (particularly the core areas of English, mathematics, science and technology, vocational curricula and skills for employability (Wolf, 2011)). At the same time more liberal views have called for localised and creative curricula (Birdwell *et al.*, 2011; Pring *et al.*, 2009; Royal Society for Arts, 2010).

Basil Bernstein's theory on the classification and framing of educational knowledge (1971) provides a unique conceptual framework within which to classify curricula according to the strength of the boundaries separating the components, and the degree of freedom teachers and pupils have to 'frame' or influence the curriculum. A.V. Kelly's 'models of curriculum planning' (2009) and Ross's (2000) curriculum typologies, provide a means of categorising curricula into types, according to their primary focus and intention, that is, whether their focus is primarily on content and transmission, on product or instrumentalism, or on process and development.

This chapter adds to the historical overview presented in Chapter 2 by considering some of the dominant influences which have impacted upon curriculum construction. It moves on to analyse the curriculum structures that emerged across the four nations as a result of developments post-1988 and especially post-political devolution in 1999. The chapter considers the relationship between these curricula and the practice of teachers, and the extent to which they constrain or stimulate innovation in learning and teaching. The conclusions address the extent to which control of the curriculum is being moved away from professionals.

Key questions for reflection

To what extent do you think a national curricula should be influenced by the needs of the economy and employability?

What other influences, if any, do you think should have an impact on a national curricula?

The structure of UK curricula in 1988

The first national curriculum in 1988 in England, Wales and Northern Ireland, and the non-statutory guidelines introduced in Scotland was perhaps an early example of what has been called 'travelling policy' (Alexiadou and Jones, 2001; Ozga and Jones, 2006) a phenomenon where policy makers exchange ideas and develop them for their national contexts. However it is also the case that in the smaller countries there were some 'hastily devised and cannily negotiated settlements' (Daugherty and Elfed-Owens, 2003, p. 251) by civil servants, as well as more inclusive processes of development and consultation, that led to modification and local adoption of the 1988 national curriculum.

The structure of the 1988 curriculum was regarded as so complex and content-heavy that in 1993 the government in England bowed to sustained criticism and instituted the Dearing Review of 1993 (named after its Chairman, Sir Ron Dearing), which was extended to Wales, and a year later to Northern Ireland. The similarity of the remit of the reviews in each of the countries (which limited the brief to reducing content, removing undue complexity and improving manageability) is further evidence of travelling policy. Such restricted terms of reference ensured that the changes represented no more than 'tinkering around the edges' (Kelly, 1999, p. 101).

The curricula introduced across the UK in 1988/9 are viewed as generally reflective of a grammar school tradition, but with some aspects of selected knowledge customised to the various nation states, for example, the Curriculum Cymreig in Wales, the various specific emphases in Northern Ireland and the greater inter-alignment of subjects within the 5–14 Curriculum in Scotland (the only one of the four curricula to be designed as non-statutory).

One of the problems with the 1988 curriculum was that all subject organisations argued for the priority of their own subjects in the curriculum. This resulted in content-heavy, largely discrete subjects in the national curriculum. One way to understand this kind of structure is through Bernstein's (1971) concept of a 'collection code' type of curriculum in which the opportunity for teachers to influence their curriculum became severely constrained.

Key questions for reflection

Is it appropriate to base a national curricula around traditional 'academic' subjects?

What are the pros and cons of national curricula organised around key skills and/or competencies?

What key skills do you think should be part of national curricula?

The structure of UK curricula: post devolution

To allow the changes resulting from the Dearing Review to become embedded a five-year moratorium on curriculum change was promised. During that time the School Curriculum and Assessment Authority (SCAA) in England initiated a public debate about the values and purposes which should inform the future curriculum. The debate was driven by concerns about:

> dominant intellectual currents (with moral relativism); the loss of moral discernment amongst the youth; the loss of respect for national leaders (temporal and spiritual); materialism and greed; the fragmentation of the family and the collapse of historic communities (through poverty and unemployment and industrial change); technological developments (resulting in a loss of control over people's lives); and the lack of a common language over morality (with a plethora of conceptions and interpretations of 'moral', 'values' and 'attitudes' and other related concepts.
>
> (SCAA, 1996, pp. 8–9)

The Chief Executive of SCAA, Dr Nick Tate, became a controversial figure in the curriculum debate which followed. At the launch of a series of consultation conferences on the relationship between 'curriculum, culture and society' in January 1996, Tate advanced four 'big ideas' about the purposes of a national curriculum. In his view the school curriculum was 'a key factor in maintaining continuity within society'; its fundamental purpose was to transmit 'an appreciation of and commitment to the best of inherited culture that has its roots in Greece and Rome, in Christianity and the many-sided traditions of European civilisation'. A key purpose of the Tate vision of the curriculum was to introduce young people to some of the characteristics of 'high culture', and he also argued that the best guarantee of minority cultures was 'a strong majority culture which values itself and which signals that traditions and customs are worthy of respect' (Ross, 2000, p. 156).

In a divided society like Northern Ireland where majority and minority cultural and religious differences had led to 30 years of violence these views proved to be a catalyst prompting calls for curriculum reform. The mood for change was energised by several factors: the historic Good Friday power-sharing agreement; the Zeitgeist associated with the approaching new millennium; pressure for education to respond to the information and technological revolution; and concerns about economic competition from an increasingly globalised economy. Proposals for radical curriculum change were advanced in 1999 informed by locally commissioned research findings including a unique longitudinal 'cohort study' of pupil's perceptions and experiences of the Common Curriculum which found pupils and teachers to be complying but not engaged with the statutory curriculum (Harland *et al.*, 2002).

In Kelly's view (2009) the prime concern of any curriculum must be its 'totality' yet the various UK national curricula had generally failed to set out a clear rationale. It was not until the English National Curriculum review of 2000 that a statement of curriculum aims and purposes first appeared, set out as three pages of introductory prose, devised after the curriculum had been reviewed and, therefore, having little impact on its

substance. Shortly afterwards Northern Ireland initiated its first major review by con-
sulting on a one-page diagrammatic curriculum framework, designed to convey the
rationale for the curriculum at a glance. The framework, when approved, was later used
as the structural basis for designing flexible minimum requirements around more succinct
process based aims, objectives and key elements, alongside a detailed framework of
thinking skills and personal capabilities. Aspects of Scotland's Curriculum for Excellence
in 2004, England's new Key Stage 3 Curriculum of 2007 and Wales' revised curriculum
of 2008 reflected similar trends.

Despite the semblance of continued policy borrowing (Raffe and Spours, 2007),
however, there is currently much greater curriculum divergence across the UK than ever
before. This can be seen, for example, in the structure and design of the various statutory
and non-statutory elements of the different UK curricula; the status, amount and detail
of content knowledge; the strength of linkages between subjects/areas of learning; the
articulation and status of thinking skills, capabilities/capacities and cross-curricular
elements; the way in which competing demands are 'designed into' curriculum structures
or remain disparate; the ways in which progression in knowledge and skills are defined;
and the power and influence of assessment and other 'strategies' to influence teaching,
learning and assessment. The trajectory of change in recent curriculum reforms in all UK
countries has been towards giving teachers (and pupils) greater flexibility to select, design
and pace learning, drawing on more flexible curriculum specifications.

However, the trend in knowledge classification is more complex. In England and
Wales, while curriculum content has been reduced, the statutory curriculum (except
during the Foundation Stages for the youngest children) remains strongly classified within
subjects and objectives driven, with potential for cross-curricular linkages remaining
external to subjects.

In Northern Ireland and Scotland common objectives/capacities exert a stronger
influence on curriculum design, with a view to improving teacher and society's understanding of broader curriculum purposes and pedagogy. In Northern Ireland, flexible
content requirements are aligned with curriculum aims and (cross-curricular) key
elements, so as to enhance the potential for linkages, while knowledge and skills outcomes
are described in very broad, generic terms, suggesting a more process-based curriculum
model.

The extent to which these developments have influenced curriculum delivery is as yet
unclear. A recent report in Wales from the schools inspection body Estyn highlighted that
few schools use the framework effectively and in general that the curriculum is still framed
by the requirements of separate subjects (Estyn, 2011a). In 2009 the Welsh Government
established a review of 8–14 educational provision which proposed that a discrete 8–14
Phase for education should be created in Wales, including a revised philosophy of the
curriculum. Whilst this was initially accepted by the Government a change in minister and
priorities in 2010 saw these proposals being at least temporarily shelved (Egan, 2009).

In Scotland detailed experiences and outcomes have been developed for each of the
eight curriculum areas, however, thinking skills have not been defined explicitly as they
have in the other three countries. While applauding the intentions and potential of a
Curriculum for Excellence a recent critique has argued that its final format represents an
uneasy mixture of Kelly's three archetypal models 'being essentially a mastery curriculum

dressed up in the language of the process model' (Priestley and Hume, 2010, p. 353). The issues that Priestley and Hume identify include the following: the four capacities remain as a set of general principles; notions of skills development, critical pedagogy and inter-disciplinary learning are generalised and remain underdeveloped; the selection of content lacks a clear rationale; there is little sense of the contested nature of knowledge; progression is at times haphazard; and its expression as potentially assessment driven outcomes may serve to restrict the development of the critical thinking and autonomy to which the curriculum aspires.

Key questions for reflection

Why do you think there appears to be a reluctance in the teaching profession to moving away from the structures and requirements of national curricula?

Curriculum and teacher pedagogy

As we have suggested the recent versions of national curriula offer teachers to varying degrees more freedom to select, sequence and pace knowledge according to the perceived needs and interests of students in order to promote higher order thinking. *Assessment for Learning* methodology has also enhanced teacher (and pupil) capacity to define appropriate learning objectives, success criteria and assessment criteria and to engage in self and peer assessment. Control over the pedagogical discourse and 'how the discourse is to be transmitted and acquired in the pedagogic context' (Bernstein, 1971) has shifted somewhat towards teachers and pupils.

Bernstein considered a number of ways in which changes in the framing of knowledge might impact on power relationships between teachers and students. The idea of co-constructing learning offers opportunities for students, for example, to influence the focus of learning, to negotiate learning criteria, to determine what is presented as evidence of proficiency, and to engage in self and peer assessment – judging their own and others' performances and owning the interpretation. These are all indicative of potentially significant shifts in power relationships between teachers and learners, towards treating pupils 'as active partners in the jointly constructed activity of learning and teaching [and in] . . . *every* aspect of schooling, not just learning itself' (Hargreaves, 2006, p. 17). The outcome is reflective of Bernstein's (1971) and Stenhouse's (1975) conception of a 'professional' model of curriculum design in which teachers and pupils have significant influence and control over the educational code and pedagogical discourse. In reality, from the onset of 1988 national curricula there has been a tension between curriculum control and teacher autonomy, and between flexibility and national prescription in thousands of school and classrooms across the UK (Alexander, 2010).

A dichotomy exists between what may be characterised at one extreme as a command and control culture in England typified by the national strategies (Docking, 2000) and, at the other extreme the far greater autonomy afforded to teachers in Scotland. The attempt to control the delivery of the curriculum in England reached a peak in the years from 1997 to 2010 when the New Labour Government imposed the National Literacy and Numeracy Strategies. This attempt to use the curriculum to achieve control over professional practice, emblematic of a belief that education performance could be improved through strong prescription and accountability, is viewed by many as counter-productive. Although school effectiveness (SE) research was one of the original drivers for the national strategies more recent SE work is arguing for the importance of teacher autonomy as one of the most powerful levers for improvement in high-performing education systems such as Finland and Ontario (Barber and Mourshed, 2007; Mourshed et al., 2010; Harris, 2006; Levin, 2008). It is something of an irony that there was compelling evidence as early as 2003 that the control and command model of the national strategies in England were not sufficiently underpinned by appropriate research and that greater variation in pedagogy was necessary (see Wyse, 2003, 2008).

Micro-control over the curriculum and teacher pedagogy, however, was not always consistently pursued and achieved even in England. In fact there were some clear contradictions in the policies pursued by the New Labour Government in this respect. One of the defining education policies of these administrations was the opening of Academies in socio-economically disadvantaged areas of England where schools (generally secondary schools) faced considerable difficulties in improving student achievement. Outside of the sacrosanct core subjects these schools were given greater licence in the way in which they met the requirements of the national curriculum. The success claimed for many of these academies has been strongly associated with the innovative approaches to curriculum they developed and the emphasis placed on creative teacher pedagogy (Shearer et al., 2007).

The extent to which national control has limited innovation is contested. Some schools have shown that it is possible, even within a restrictive national curriculum framework, to have innovation as result of teacher professionalism leading to success for students. The ability to do this in primary and secondary schools in Cambridgeshire, for example, was described by Hart et al. (2004). Ofsted have highlighted the extent to which many successful primary schools in England, faced by challenging socio-economic circumstances, have been able to adapt the curriculum and to achieve success through high quality teaching (Ofsted, 2009). Studies in Wales have pointed to the same conclusions (James et al., 2006; Welsh Assembly Government, 2005). In these cases the curriculum is not seen as a constraint on successful practice, but the issue of teacher confidence and quality is highlighted. Where teachers are well trained and professionally developed they are able to use the curriculum as a tool to achieve success. But others argue that the accountability and performativity culture (particulary high stakes testing such as national statutory tests) has very strongly influenced headteachers and other key players in the education system (Alexander, 2010; Claxton, 2008).

A study in Scotland indicated very strongly that teachers mediated curriculum direction and guidance in relation to their own existing practice (Hulme et al., 2009). In their research for the Cambridge Primary Review, Wyse et al. (2010) found evidence of contested versions of the extent that national control impacted on teacher innovation. There was research supporting considerable change in practice as a result of the periods of intense national control but also research showing that in spite of what are regarded by some as superficial changes continuity in practice continued. Wyse *et al.* (2010) concluded that the national strategies had a significant influence on practice. Mediation of the curriculum by teachers can be viewed as an understandable assertion of their professionalism, or as resistance to change and 'anti-professional'. A report from the inspectorate in Wales highlighted these tensions in relation to the successful development of the Foundation Phase curriculum in primary schools (Estyn, 2011b).

The transmission of curriculum structures and requirements into professional practice is not a straightforward linear process; it is a multi-faceted, contested, dynamic process. The role of the curriculum in successful school education is more profound than politicians, curriculum developers and policy makers understand. The curriculum is often strongly influenced by teacher pedagogy and autonomy, but since 1988 this autonomy has been come under pressure and been constrained by the the assessment and accountability systems.

Key questions for reflection

Why do you think it is that in some of the most apparently successful education systems in the world, there are very limited national curricula?

To what extent could it be argued that the curriculum should be the servant of outstanding learning and teaching rather than the master?

Conclusions

We have shown in this chapter that the school curriculum remains a highly significant aspect of education. For some it represents the vehicle for transmission of a nation's culture to its young. However one of the questions that we have asked in this chapter is, who decides which particular aspects of the culture are to be the focus of national curricula? The chapter also identified a number of risks that occur when elite groups make decisions about the curriculum on behalf of citizens. On the one hand education systems are struggling to understand and respond to dominant macro influences while at the same time attempting to reflect some deeply symbolic national values. As Stephen Ball said:

> Both historically and currently there are significant differences between the English education system and English education policy and the rest of the UK . . . While Scotland, Wales and Northern Ireland are not exempt from the pressures of globalisation, they mediate those pressures differently; they balance them differently against other priorities and face different social and economic problems.
>
> (2008, p. 2)

The idea of travelling policy and its influence on national curricula is now clearly recognised although its implications continue to need research. It appears that some big ideas, such as the asserted need for top-down control through national frameworks, remain prevalent. At the same time the most recent curriculum policy seems to be built on what appears to be grudging acceptance that levels of local control over curricula are vital to sustain professional engagement and to impact positively on pupils' learning.

Areas of local control of curricula are opening up, but paradoxically at a time when international and national assessment and testing systems are exerting ever greater influence (see Chapter 5, this volume). A pressing question is the extent to which teachers, particularly those new to the profession, have the capacity to take the freedoms that are being offered and innovate in ways that will bring a long needed dynamism back to the majority of schools and classrooms, not the few.

The insights in this chapter illustrate how countries in very close proximity to each other have had ideas imposed from the centre, have borrowed ideas from each other, and yet have interpreted and implemented them differently as a consequence of a number of factors, for example: the pressures and aspirations of political context; professional relationships between national centres and the periphery; differing emphases on aspects such as skills development and cross-curricular learning, and attitudes to teacher professionalism. The analysis suggests that national context remains a strong factor in UK education, and local control of the curriculum for pupils and teachers remains a battle to be won.

Teacher education/training task

Discuss the extent to which the national curricula in the four nations exert control over the daily work of teachers and pupils.

Further reading

Alexander, R. (ed.) (2010) *Children, their World, their Education*. Abingdon: Routledge.
   The outcome of the extensive Cambridge Primary Review. Confined to consideration of the curriculum in England but, nevertheless, a comprehensive review of the issues covered in this chapter.
Bernstein, B. (1971) 'On the Classification and Framing of Education Knowledge', in Young, M. (ed.) *Knowledge and Control: New Directions for the Sociology of Education*. London: Routledge, pp. 47–69.
   Full coverage of the classification approach to curricula set out in this chapter from one of the most profound thinkers on the role of curriculum within education.
James, C., Connolly, M., Dunning, G. and Elliot, T. (2006) *How Very Effective Primary Schools Work*. London: Paul Chapman Publishing.
   A study of how effective primary schools succeed in using the national curriculum to produce high quality learning, teaching and student achievement. Based on extensive case studies drawn from primary schools in disadvantaged areas of Wales.

References

Alexander, R. (ed.) (2010) *Children, their World, their Education*. Abingdon: Routledge.
Alexiadou, N. and Jones, K. (2001) 'Travelling Policy/Local Spaces', paper to the Congress Marx International 111 Le Capitale et L'Humanite University of Paris X, 26–29 September.

Ball, S.J. (1993) 'What is Policy? Texts, Trajectories and Toolboxes'. *Discourse* 13 (2), 10–17.

Ball, S.J. (1997) 'Policy Sociology and Critical Social Research: *A Personal Review of Recent Education Policy and Policy Research*'. British Educational Research Journal 23 (3), 257–274.

Ball, S.J. (2008) *The Education Debate: Policy and Politics in the Twenty-First Century.* Bristol: Policy Press.

Barber, M. (2007) *Instruction to Deliver.* London: Politico's.

Barber, M. and Mourshed, M. (2007) *How the World's Best Performing School Systems Came Out On Top.* McKinsey and Company.

Bernstein, B. (1971) 'On the Classification and Framing of Education Knowledge', in Young, M. (ed.) *Knowledge and Control: New Directions for the Sociology of Education.* London: Routledge, pp. 47–69.

Birdwell, J., Grist, M. and Margo, J. (2011) *The Forgotten Half.* London: Demos.

Bowe, R., Ball, S.J. and Gold, A. (1992) *Reforming Education and Changing Schools.* London: Routledge.

Cassen, R. and Kingdon, G. (2007) *Tackling Low Educational Achievement.* York: Joseph Rowntree Foundation.

Claxton, G. (2008) *What's The Point of School.* Oxford: One World.

Daugherty, R. and Elfed-Owens, P. (2003) 'A National Curriculum for Wales: A Case Study of Education Policy-Making in the Era of Administrative Devolution'. *British Journal of Educational Studies* 53 (3), 233–253.

Docking, J. (2000) 'Curriculum Initiatives', in Docking, J. (ed.) *New Labour's Policies for Schools.* London: David Fulton, pp. 61–76.

Egan, D. (2009) *Report of the Welsh Assembly Government Task and Finish Group on 8–14 Education in Wales.* Cardiff: Welsh Assembly Government.

Estyn (2011a) *An Evaluation of the Impact of the Non-Statutory Skills Framework for 3–19 Year Olds in Wales at Key Stage 2.* Cardiff: Estyn.

Estyn (2011b) *Literacy and the Foundation Phase.* Cardiff: Estyn.

Fullan, M. (2010) *All Systems Go: The Change Imperative for Whole System Reform.* Thousand Oaks: Corwin.

Gale, T. (2001) 'Critical Policy Sociology: Historiography, Archaeology and Genealogy as Methods of Policy Analysis'. *Journal of Education Policy* 16 (5), 379–393.

Goodman, A. and Gregg, P. (2010) *Poorer Children's Educational Attainment: How Important Are Attitudes and Behaviour?* York: Joseph Rowntree Foundation.

Gutman, L. and Akerman, R. (2008) *Determinants of Aspirations.* London: Centre for Research on the Wider Benefits of Learning.

Hargreaves, D.H. (2006) *A New Shape for Schooling.* London: Specialist Schools and AcademiesTrust/iNET.

Harland, J., Moor, H., Kinder, K. and Ashworth, M. (2002). *Is the Curriculum Working?* The Key Stage 3 Phase of the Northern Ireland Curriculum Cohort Study. Slough: NFER.

Harris, J. (2006) *Alignment in Finland.* Melbourne: Educational Alignments.

Hart, S., Dixon, A., Drummond, M.J. and McIntyre, D. (2004) *Learning Without Limits.* Maidenhead: Open University Press.

Hulme, M., Baumfield, V., Livingston, K. and Menter, I. (2009) 'The Scottish Curriculum in Transition: Curriculum for Excellence'. Paper given at British Educational Research Association Annual Conference, Manchester, September 2009.

Kelly, A.V. (2009) *The Curriculum: Theory and Practice,* 6th Edition. London: Sage (first published 1977).

James, C., Connolly, M., Dunning, G. and Elliot, T. (2006) *How Very Effective Primary Schools Work.* London: Paul Chapman Publishing.

Leitch, S. (2006) *Prosperity for All in the Global Economy – World Class Skills.* Norwich: HMSO.

Levin, B. (2008) *How To Change 5000 Schools.* Cambridge, MA: Harvard Education Press.

McKinsey and Company (2009) *The Economic Impact of the Achievement Gap in America's Schools*. McKinsey and Company.

Mourshed, M., Chijioke, C. and Barber, M. (2010) *How the World's Most Improved School Systems Keep Getting Better*. London: McKinsey and Company.

Mundy, K. (2005) *Globalisation and Educational Change, New Policy Worlds*, International Handbook on Educational Policy. Springer Publications

OECD (2010) *The High Cost of Low Educational Performance*. Paris: OECD.

Ofsted (2009) *Twenty Outstanding Primary Schools Excelling Against the Odds*. London: Ofsted.

Ozga, J. and Jones, R. (2006) 'Travelling and Embedded Policy: The Case of Knowledge Transfer'. *Journal of Education Policy* 21 (1), 1–17.

Priestley, M. (2002) 'Global Discourses and National Reconstruction: The Impact of Globalization on Curriculum Policy'. *Curriculum Journal* 13 (1), 121–138.

Priestley, M. and Hume, W. (2010) 'The Development of Scotland's Curriculum for Excellence: Amnesia and Déjà Vu'. *Oxford Review of Education* 36 (3), 345–361.

Pring, R., Hayward, G., Hodgson, A., Johnson, J., Keepo, E., Oancea, A., Rees, G., Spours, K. and Wilde, S. (2009) *Education for All*. Abingdon: Routledge.

Raffe, D. and Spours, K. (2007) 'Three Models of Policy Learning and Policy-Making in 14–19 Education', in Raffe, D. and Spours, K. (eds) *Policy-Making and Policy Learning in 14–19 Education*, pp. 1–32. London: IoE London.

Rizvi, F. and Lingard, B. (2010) *Globalizing Education Policy*. Oxford: Routledge.

Ross, A. (2000) *Curriculum Construction and Critique*. Oxford: Routledge.

Royal Society for Arts (2010) *The RSA Area Based Curriculum: Engaging the Local*. London: Royal Society for Arts.

Schools Curriculum and Assessment Authority (1996) *Education for Adult Life: The Spiritual and Moral Development of Young People*. London: Schools Curriculum and Assessment Authority.

Shearer, G., Vacher, K. and Hargreaves, D.H. (2007) *System Redesign 3: Curriculum Redesign*. London: Specialist Schools and Academies Trust.

Stenhouse, L. (1975) *An Introduction to Curriculum Research and Development*. London: Open University Press.

Welsh Assembly Government (2005) *Narrowing the Gap in the Performance of Schools Project: Phase 2 Primary Schools*. Cardiff: Welsh Assembly Government.

Wolf, A. (2011) *Review of Vocational Education*. London: Department for Education.

Wyse, D. (2003) 'The National Literacy Strategy: A Critical Review of Empirical Evidence'. *British Educational Research Journal* 29 (6), 903–916.

Wyse, D. (2008) 'Primary Education: Who's in Control?'. *Education Review* 21 (1), 76–82.

Wyse, D., McCreery, E. and Torrance, H. (2010) 'The Trajectory and Impact of National Reform: Curriculum and Assessment in English Primary Schools', in Alexander, R., Doddington, C., Gray, J., Hargreaves, L. and Kershner, R. (eds) *The Cambridge Primary Review Research Surveys*. London: Routledge.

Chapter 7

Languages and literacy

Dominic Wyse

Chapter summary

As the first of three chapters with a cross-curricular focus this chapter explores the place of language and literacy in the curriculum. The chapter begins with an account of the English language internationally. This is followed by reflections on the nature of spoken language, particularly in relation to multilingualism. These two sections that reveal linguistic diversity are followed by a set of linguistic principles that are used to underpin the interdisciplinary accounts of research on reading and writing in the chapter. The fascinating variations in the language requirements in the curricula of Northern Ireland, Scotland and Wales are analysed, particularly in relation to their general organisation, and the ways that talk, reading and writing are represented. The chapter concludes by arguing that linguistic diversity and pupils' rights and voices should be two central organising features of language curricula.

Language is often regarded as the most important area of the curriculum. There are a number of features about language that contribute to its importance: 1) being literate is regarded as necessary for life, and necessary to access all other curriculum areas; 2) there is a close link between language and identity: this personal connection often results in strong views about the subject; 3) politicians have increasingly linked literacy levels in children and adults with national prosperity. Hence language is also an area that causes controversy, something that is particularly the case with English in the curriculum.

One important consideration when thinking about language curricula (or any curricula for that matter) is the extent that research evidence and appropriate theory can be seen to be reflected in curriculum texts, guidance and classroom practice. Language is an area that has attracted a wealth of research over the last 20 years, and this research offers some clear indications about appropriate curriculum and pedagogy. In view of the wealth of evidence available this chapter begins by outlining some key ideas built on such research and theory. It then uses some of these key ideas to guide its analysis of the language sections in national curriculum texts in the four nations.

One of the most important changes to the context for language and literacy in the curriculum of different countries has been the global growth in the use of English as a language. The growth of English is played out in the contexts of continent, country, state, district, city, town, school and classroom. This global phenomenon may seem a somewhat distant idea in relation to the daily lives of pupils and teachers in the UK. But if you pause to consider the language backgrounds and experiences of the pupils in any class then these issues have a direct bearing (for research evidence on this see Wyse *et al.*, 2011). Another reason why consideration of the broader aspects of language is important is that effective teaching is informed by appropriate knowledge. Part of this knowledge is as full an understanding of language as possible. This includes the international dimensions coupled with appropriate linguistic principles to guide practice.

In all cities in the UK, and in many rural areas, there are populations of students who are multilingual. The range is broadest in London contrasting with the larger homogenous communities in other cities who have, for example, British Asian origins. If we look globally, in the continent of Africa every country has a different socio-political engagement with English. For example, the 13 languages enshrined in South African law contrast with the twin focus on Kiswahili and English in Tanzania. In primary schools in Tanzania Kiswahili is the medium used for teaching; in secondary schools English is used. In other African countries the influence of French and Dutch colonialists provides different contexts for English. In Scandinavian countries the success of English language teaching supported by the use of European language frameworks is tempered by popular concerns that national languages may be endangered (Simensen, 2010). China and the Chinese language is also of particular interest, in its own right and in relation to the spread of English. Bolton (2003) reminds us that the early seventeenth century was the beginning of contact between speakers of English and speakers of Chinese.

Bolton (2003) also raises the issue of total numbers of speakers of Chinese and English. Arriving at accurate figures is complex (Crystal, 2010). The first problem is the world population growth of about 1.2 per cent per annum which means that figures for less-developed nations change rapidly. Even in more stable populations, acquiring information is difficult when most census questionnaires do not include questions about linguistic background. Even if you can ask people about their language(s) there are difficulties in relation to measuring proficiency of language use, the way that people name their languages versus other forms of language such as dialect, and political pressure to conform to particular ideas about the place of certain languages. Accepting these caveats Crystal (2010) estimated that the figures for numbers of speakers in 2010 were as follows:

English, in countries where people are regularly exposed to English, including learning
    English in school 2,902,853,000
English, second language speakers 1,800,000,000
Chinese, mother tongue, all languages 1,071,000,000
Mandarin Chinese, mother tongue 726,000,000
English, mother tongue 427,000,000.

A further problem for estimating the growing use of English is that there are no figures available for people who have learned English as a foreign language in countries where

English does not have special status (including in China where anecdotal accounts suggest that the number of people learning English has grown dramatically). Halliday (2003) recognised English as a global language and made a distinction between this global spread and international variants of English that result from the spread. Crystal (2000) saw the possibility of an international standard English with local and national variants. The spread of English, just like any language, is an organic process that is impervious to attempts to divert it.

If we accept that multiple linguistic influences, including different languages, are a feature of all societies then there are implications for teaching and learning. One of the most important implications is how we should understand the multilingualism that all pupils will experience and/or encounter in their lives. As part of his *developmental interdependence hypothesis* and other work Cummins (1979) proposed that the particular features of school discourse, such as the emphasis on particular forms of literacy learning, are part of what can make things difficult for bilingual pupils. Cummins' main conclusion was that support for bilingual pupils is necessary and there is a need to include assessments of pupils' language and literacy understanding in order to provide the most appropriate pedagogy. Reese *et al.*'s study (2000) carried out in the United States with Spanish/English speaking pupils provided support for some elements of Cummins' theories. Their most significant finding was that even if parents were not able to speak the US's first language, English, and therefore used a second language (Spanish), parents' engagement with books and reading with their children was beneficial for their children's learning to read in the *first* language and their education more generally. Research clearly shows that support for home languages benefits the learning of another language, and that impeding the use of home languages is damaging. This is supported by recent neuroscience work. For example, Kovelman *et al.*'s (2008) research showed that bilinguals have differentiated representations in the brain of their two languages. They also found no evidence to suggest that exposure to two languages might be a source of fundamental and persistent language confusion.

I have addressed global aspects of the English language and theories of bilingualism, but further selection of linguistic theory relevant to a consideration of curriculum requires principles that can delimit and focus the areas of most relevance to teaching. The following principles were derived from analysis of the linguistic and pedagogic aspects of three publications, one aimed at researchers and policy makers (Wyse *et al.*, 2010), one aimed at researchers (Wyse, 2011) and the other aimed at teachers (Wyse and Jones, 2008). The linguistic principles that underpin the teaching of English, language and literacy (TELL) are as follows:

- Communication of understandable meaning is the driving force of language.
- Analysis of language in use is the basis for appropriate knowledge for pupils and teachers.
- As a consequence of the natural processes of language change descriptive accounts of language are more appropriate than prescriptive accounts.
- Experiencing and reflecting on the processes of reading and writing are an important resource to enhance teaching and learning.
- Language and social status (or power) are inextricably linked.

Further explanation and examples of these principles in practice can be found in Wyse (2011). In the sections on reading and writing below these principles have served to provide a linguistic backdrop for the account.

Key questions for reflection

How might the linguistic principles listed in this chapter affect your selection of texts for activities in the classroom?

Reading

The texts that children choose to read and that teachers select to inspire children are a vital part of language in the curriculum. But also of importance is how we might view the processes or *transactions* that take place when children engage with texts. As Rosenblatt (1985, p. 100) says,

> we need to see the reading act as an event involving a particular individual and a particular text, happening at a particular time, under particular circumstances, in a particular social and cultural setting, and as part of the ongoing life of the individual and the group.

Rosenblatt argued that her notion of the transaction was not the same as the separation of text and reader that is a feature of cognitive views of transaction that include information processing models. For example psychologists look at what they call reading comprehension in a rather different way to Rosenblatt's transactions, and yet both shed light on the same reading processes.

Irrespective of the preferred way of thinking about reading processes, unless someone is motivated to read then learning to read is less likely to happen. Wigfield and Guthrie (1997) found that children's motivation for reading was correlated with the amount and breadth of their reading. They also found that intrinsic motivation predicted more strongly amount and breadth than extrinsic motivation. The implications of these findings for supporting children are first and foremost the importance of encouraging children's motivation, for example by providing texts that are likely to interest them. However, there is of course a dilemma in relation to intrinsic motivation. When does encouragement to read by teachers become extrinsic motivation? This implies a subtle balanced between the *requirement* to read, and *encouragement* to read. Text transactions, then, involve cognitive and socio-cultural factors but what happens over time as reading develops? Stanovich (1986) characterised different amounts of reading experience as the rich getting richer and the poor getting poorer. He showed that there are gains for vocabulary growth and reading skill attributable to increased volume of reading alone, so those children who do not experience enough opportunities to read are at a disadvantage.

Although important developments have taken place in reading research, once attention turns to how research might inform the teaching of reading a further series of complexities arise. The tension between research, recommendations for teaching, and teaching policy on reading has been at the centre of some of the fiercest debates about education, so much so that it has sometimes even been called 'the great debate' (Chall, 1983). In brief, the argument centres on a difference of opinion about how children learn to read and how they should be taught. When this is played out in the media, polarised positions are suggested and an unhelpful simplification of what is a complex picture often emerges. However it is the case that at the heart of the arguments is a basic difference of beliefs. Some people have as a core belief that the main thrust of reading teaching should be 'top-down', where the whole text is the starting point and teaching about smaller linguistic elements such as words, syllables, alphabet, etc., follows from the whole text (not to be confused with top-down in relation to policy development that we talk about throughout this book). Others believe that teaching reading should be mainly oriented to 'bottom-up', by focusing on teaching the alphabetic code first and foremost and that this will lead to reading comprehension. These opposing beliefs have also been linked with particular approaches to the teaching of reading. For example the *whole language* approach in the United States or the *real book approach* in the UK have been linked with top-down, and *synthetic phonics* has been linked with bottom-up. A questionable assumption, made by some, is that whole language teaching does not involve phonics instruction, but as Dahl *et al.* (1999) show, that this is not necessarily the case. They challenge the idea that systematic phonics instruction must be a predetermined sequence of skills, and provide evidence that whole language teaching can be effective.

Overall, what the research evidence shows is that engagement with whole texts *and* teaching of the alphabetic code are important (Wyse, 2010). Reading research over the last 20 years has clearly demonstrated the importance of knowledge about letters and phonemes (sounds) as a small but vital part of learning to read, but although children can learn to read without systematic phonics (Durkin, 1966; Clarke, 1976; Wyse, 2007) they cannot learn to read without engaging with whole texts.

A further difficulty with translating research evidence into classroom practice has been the lack of attention paid by some researchers to the realities and complexities of classroom practice. For example, an important strand of research evidence comes from analysis of teacher–pupil interaction. Given that all teaching is mediated through dialogue between teachers and pupils this is an important element of any consideration of effectiveness of teaching. Working in this area, Juzwik *et al.* (2008) identify the importance of what they called oral narrative events. Effective teaching encouraged pupils to share 'small stories' about their lives and things that interested them. Teachers can encourage this oral narrative by emphasising open conversation as part of teaching.

Another feature of classroom practice is the fact that teachers are faced with pupils who differ markedly in their experience of reading: their understanding, their attainment and their knowledge. This is the realm of *differentiation*, including children who struggle with reading and those who learn to read earlier than most. The work of Marie Clay, which focused on children with reading difficulties (Clay, 1979), is internationally renowned. Clay argued that early intervention was vital to help children with reading difficulties. In the New Zealand context, where she did her early work, she said that if a child was not reading by age six then extra support was required. Unlike many programmes aimed at supporting children with reading difficulties, Clay's *reading recovery* lesson (a 30-minute one-to-one session between teacher and pupil) begins with the reading of whole texts and progresses to letter work before finishing with reading of whole text. Even greater effects for Clay's approach have been found with the inclusion of systematic phonics rather than the letter work that Clay originally intended. Although there have been differences of opinion about the effectiveness of Clay's methods there is unusually strong research evidence from a range of countries to support it (D'Agostino and Murphy, 2004).

At the other end of the differentiation spectrum are precocious children who read at home before formal education begins. Durkin (1966) in the United States, and Clarke (1976) in the UK, researched the factors that led to these children being able to read so early. One of the most important factors was having parents who took an active interest in their children's learning and who engaged in interaction that was conducive to learning. There was also evidence that parents' support tended to be non-systematic. This evidence clearly shows, once again, that some children do not need systematic phonics in order to learn to read. The implications for teachers are that systematic phonics teaching will be required for most children but not all, therefore reading teaching has to be differentiated.

Key questions for reflection

Discuss the key differences between your approach to the teaching of reading and that of one of your peers. Relate one of your differences to the research evidence reviewed in this chapter.

Writing

The concept of *emergent literacy* came about due to growing interest in young children's learning and a dissatisfaction with deficit theories. Deficit theories are basically negative ways of thinking about children and their development. For example, the phrase 'they've got no language' about particular groups of children is a deficit theory. It is inaccurate because all children develop language. Clay's work was influential (in addition to her contribution to reading, see above) in recognising that children's early attempts at mark-making are a form of writing distinguished only by lack of experience and understanding rather than a form of non-writing (see also Bradford and Wyse, 2010). In everyday language some people refer to 'scribble' rather than seeing young children's mark-making as 'writing'. Yang and Noel identified the common patterns of mark-making in four- and five-year-old children and noted the importance of drawing as a contributor to writing development. For emergent writers, writing their own name is a very important part of their emergent literacy. Bloodgood (1999) showed how name writing was linked to a range of important early literacy learning. Links were found between name writing and learning of the alphabetic code, although individual children differed in the extent to which they could form letters and/or name letters. It was theorised that learning the alphabetic code and name writing reinforced each other.

A key area of debate with regard to writing has been the distinction between the processes of writing and the products and forms of writing. Although Graves' (1975) original research received some criticism (e.g. Smagorinsky, 1987), there are few who doubt the influence his ideas had in practice, particularly in the United States. Graves articulated the *process approach* to writing, the key features of which are: generation of writing topics by pupils; regular writing workshops; 'publishing' in the classroom; teacher–pupil writing conferences; skills teaching in 'mini lessons' and embedded in one-to-one support for pupils' writing. Wyse's (1988) early research focused on the process approach and showed the ways that teachers integrated some of the ideas of the process approach with other approaches (including more 'structured' teaching). He showed that this integration of teaching approaches was a particular characteristic of the teaching of writing in England at the time.

A challenge to the process approach came from those who felt that the approach was too informal and that teaching of written genres needed to be more systematic. Since that time clear evidence of the challenges for pupils of what is called 'argumentative' writing has continued to emerge (Andrews *et al.*, 2006; Yeh, 1998). An important consideration for teaching writing is how to strike the appropriate balance between an emphasis on teaching and supporting composition, as opposed to the transcription elements such as spelling, grammar and handwriting.

The importance of processes, environments, ownership, etc., for writing combined with individual children's cognitive development are perhaps implicitly evident in recent empirical work on effective teaching of writing. Research such as that by Graham (2006) has provided experimental trial evidence that the combination of a focus on writing processes, and instruction for writing strategics, is the most effective way to teach writing. As Wyse and Jones (2008) explain, pupil ownership (that is related to motivation) is the other vital aspect of such writing teaching.

If phonics has often been the catalyst to ignite debate on the teaching of reading then grammar, to a lesser intensity, has done the same for writing. Historically there was once a time when grammar teaching was the sine qua non of English teaching. In modern times it has been seen by some as an essential and dominant requirement to help pupils' writing. Work by Wyse (2001) (confirmed by Andrews *et al.* (2004) in their systematic review and meta-analysis) clearly showed that decontextualised teaching of grammar to improve writing was ineffective. A theoretical reason for this was explored in research on pupils' explanations for use of non-standard (or 'incorrect' in common parlance) grammar. Wyse (2006) found that language use, at sentence and word level, was influenced by pupils' thinking about semantic elements at text level, which led to the use of non-standard grammar. The study provided evidence of the need for contextualised writing teaching for improving pupils' use of written language.

The transcription elements of writing continue to attract significant attention, particularly spelling. A seemingly minor point, but one that in fact turns out to be significant, is the decision by teachers, early years' workers, and parents, about whether to use letters' names to identify letters, or common sounds to identify letters. Treiman *et al.* (2008) provide evidence that children use letters' names as a source to help them learn about sounds. Another feature of transcription is the nature of the tools that are used in order to compose, or *design*. The *new literacies* movement is in part concerned with technological change. Continuing interest in multiliteracies and multimodality has prompted debate between those who see the need for greater theoretical exploration and those who argue that it is time to research what kinds of teaching, involving new technologies, is likely to support children's learning more effectively (for different views see Jewitt and Kress, 2010 and Reinking, 2010). My own view is that new technologies are simply tools that still require the age-old capacities to compose text and compose visual images in order to communicate meanings that satisfy the composer and the reader. Alvermann (2008) is quite right in her argument that new technologies used by pupils at home cannot simply be ignored in school.

The first section of this chapter has revealed just a small selection of some of the extensive research and scholarship that has transformed our understanding of language and literacy. Although the issues are complex, there is powerful evidence to inform evidence-based curriculum policy development. There are, of course, still many areas where research has not yet provided sufficient evidence relevant to policy and classroom practice. These areas provide ideal opportunities for teacher-led curriculum development that can feed into future research.

The next section of the chapter builds on some of the themes evident in the theory and research, and applies these to a comparison of language curricula in the four nations.

Key questions for reflection

Agree a list of five factors that are likely to improve writing teaching in the classroom with a small group of your peers.

Language in national curricula

In England the national curriculum subject of English caused controversy with politicians from its inception (Cox, 1991). The inclusion of 'speaking and listening' in the curriculum was testament to the growing conviction that oral language was a neglected feature of the curriculum in England. More controversial was the requirement to teach 'standard English', as this suggested to many a deficit view of most pupils' language. In the different versions of the national curriculum from 1999 to 2012 pupils had to be taught some of the main features of standard English but also that speech could vary in different contexts. The main sections of speaking and listening, reading, and writing in the 1999 version of the national curriculum were sub-divided into knowledge, skills and understanding, and breadth of study. The emphasis on 'phonemic awareness and phonic knowledge' had been greatly strengthened in comparison to the 1988 version of the national curriculum, reflecting intense debate about the teaching of reading that led to the implementation of the national literacy strategy (NLS) in 1997. The changes to phonic knowledge reflected convenient alignment with the *framework for teaching* that was part of the NLS, indeed the national curriculum explicitly referred to the NLS framework for teaching as the detailed account of how to teach reading and writing. The requirements for writing in the 1999 national curriculum appropriately focused first and foremost on composition within a process of planning and drafting. The transcription elements of punctuation, spelling, handwriting and presentation followed, suggesting that they were there to support the composition of writing. Between 1997 and 2010, the implementation of the NLS only served to exacerbate tensions around the subject of English. One of the major problems was the omission of talk from the framework of teaching objectives that covered reading and writing (Department for Education and Employment (DfEE), 1998; Department for Education and Skills (DfES), 2007), a surprising omission in view of the hard-won place of speaking and listening in the original national curriculum.

In 2011 the review of the national curriculum in England was in progress, and the early signs were that some familiar debates were recurring. Not least the decision to structure the curriculum as subjects rather than other organisational devices such as areas of learning. Another potentially contentious area was the suggestion from some politicians that a canon of literature should be specified as required reading. An area on which there was wholly inadequate consultation was the mandatory use of *synthetic phonics*, and particularly controversial a national phonics test for six-year-olds, in the face of evidence showing the potential risks of this policy (Wyse and Goswami, 2008).

An analysis of the language requirements in the national curriculum texts in Northern Ireland, Scotland and Wales reveals fascinating differences from each other and from England (Council for the Curriculum Examinations and Assessment (CCEA), 2007; Department for Children, Education, Lifelong Learning and Skills, 2008; Scottish Government, 2011). Northern Ireland titles the subject area, *language and literacy*. The preamble to the subject requirements for the foundation stage makes it clear that children come to school with language experience that teachers need to build on. The preamble for the later key stages also includes reference to developing children's understanding of language through reflections on their mother tongue and other languages. The language and literacy requirements are divided into talking and listening, reading and writing. The holistic, contextualised nature of the introductory sections are different in character to what are called the statutory requirements. These begin with 'attention and listening skills' (p. 18) and 'phonological awareness', which come before the 'social use of language'. It is unusual to see phonological awareness included as a language requirement rather than as a reading requirement.

As far as reading is concerned the development of a 'love of books' (p. 20) in children is the first priority for the foundation stage. In the later key stages this becomes an emphasis on developing individual tastes and preferences. The statutory requirements emphasise 'modelled, shared, paired and guided reading' and reading a range of texts for enjoyment and information. Skills and knowledge are appropriately located within the holistic context of meaningful engagement with texts. The requirements for writing similarly have an appropriate emphasis on the purposes of writing and its composition.

Scotland's *Curriculum for Excellence* specifies its subject requirements through the *Experiences and Outcomes. Literacy across Learning* is specified as one of three major areas of responsibility for practitioners (health and wellbeing, and numeracy across learning are the other two). The political links between social identity and economic factors as part of language can be seen in the very first sentence of the literacy across learning section: 'Language and literacy are of personal, social and economic importance' (Scottish Government, 2011, p. 20). Notably, this section also provides a definition of literacy: '*the set of skills which allows an individual to engage fully in society and in learning, through the different forms of language, and the range of texts, which society values and finds useful'* (p. 20; italics in original).

The Scottish curriculum titles its subject section as *Languages*. Uniquely this includes the following five major sections: *Classical languages; Gaelic (learners); Literacy and English; Literacy and Gàidhlig; and Modern Languages*. A distinction is made between the learning of Gaelic for pupils who are new or relatively new to Gaelic, and the place of Gàidhlig (Scottish Gaelic) as full bilingual use of the language including as a medium of instruction. These two sections represent a powerful political statement about language and Scottish identity. The inclusion of classical languages is a radical idea. It is made clear that the purpose of classical language study is to develop awareness of culture and heritage. The study of classical languages begins for pupils at the secondary school stage.

In the *experiences and outcomes* element of the curriculum the five major sections are all divided up into the *organisers* of listening and talking, reading, and writing ('mode' might have been a more appropriate description in relation to language). The requirements are preceded by a list of aspects that pupils are expected to have opportunities to engage with. These include, 'engage with and create a wide range of texts' (p. 24). An interesting feature of the language of these aspects and the requirements more generally is the use of the personal pronoun 'I', implying that the curriculum is pupil-centred. For example, 'I develop and extend my literacy skills when I have opportunities to: communicate, collaborate and build relationships' (p. 24). Another interesting feature is the *Enjoyment and choice* strand which is the first column in the first section of the tables that are used to organise the requirements for each organiser. However, the first statement for listening and talking in the early years is about learning about the patterns and sounds of language. Perhaps the second statement in this column, 'I enjoy exploring and choosing stories . . .' would have been better placed first, to clearly signal that experience with whole texts is foremost, and that these experiences are supported by a range of understandings, including phonological understanding. These two statements about sounds of language and exploring stories, and their sequence, are repeated in the same place in the reading section (and in the writing section). It is not clear that either enjoyment or choice are very well represented by a requirement for learning about sounds.

For writing, the requirements in the primary education stages include, 'I enjoy creating texts of my choice and I regularly select subject, purpose, format and resources to suit the needs of my audience' (p. 33). This is indeed a powerful statement. The opportunity for pupils to choose what to write (in the fullest sense including topic, form and ways of working) is something that has very rarely been seen in practice since the process writing approach of the 1990s (Wyse, 1998). Like Northern Ireland, Scotland's national curriculum texts include extensive descriptions of the rationales for the experiences and outcomes material and its organisation. Taken as a whole the texts that describe Curriculum for Excellence are numerous, perhaps too numerous.

Wales titles its subject *Language, literacy and communication skills* at the Foundation Phase level (Department for Children, Education, Lifelong Learning and Skills, 2008). The addition of 'communication' is perhaps intended to signal a link with the additional *Skills framework*, that is a separate text but is part of the curriculum in Wales. It is notable that

Wales' requirements for talk are called 'Oracy'. This seems more appropriate than 'speaking and listening', after all curricula do not have the equivalent phrase reading and *viewing*, but 'talking' or 'talk' is surely the most natural way to describe this aspect of the curriculum.

Wales' curriculum is fully bilingual as can be seen in the inclusion of the *Welsh Language Development* section. However, rather than see linguistic diversity as the norm, pupils are only expected to 'show positive attitudes to speakers of languages other than Welsh and English' (p. 19) although it is expected that learning in other languages should inform first language development. The requirements are succinct with only the two sections of 'skills' and 'range' for each mode of oracy, reading and writing. The first requirement for reading is for children to enjoy reading. The smaller aspects of language, such as phonological understanding, come later but there is recognition that semantic and syntactic understand are also important as reading 'skills'. The writing section similarly has a whole text focus with an emphasis on 'mark-making' (p. 21b) first, and alphabetic knowledge coming subsequently.

Wales locates its national curriculum, and indeed its education policy in general, within the framework of the UN Convention on the Rights of the Child (CRC). Consistent with this, at key stage two (age 7 to 11) the subject *English* begins with a statement of the importance of respecting children's rights and ensuring that all children are included in the education of the curriculum. Unlike the foundation stage curriculum, phonic skills are the first requirement for reading 'skills', although consistent with the foundation stage these are seen as being used alongside semantic and syntactic knowledge within a 'balanced and coherent programme' (p. 13). The genres of writing are the first focus in the writing skills section but unlike Scotland there is no sense that pupils might have extensive choice over their writing, in spite of the CRC article that gives children the right to be consulted on all matters that affect them.

Key questions for reflection

Select one of the articles of the UN Convention on the Rights of the Child and consider how it might relate to the teaching of language or literacy.

Implications for language teaching and future curricula

The national curricula in the four nations have in common the recognition of the importance of language for learning and teaching. Language in the curriculum is an area that is affected more than most other curriculum areas by cultural and political influences, for example the place of Gaelic in the Scottish curriculum, and bilingualism in the Welsh and Irish curricula. But none of the curricula analysed in this chapter explicitly recognise and build sufficiently on the wider linguistic diversity that is the reality of many communities in the UK. One of the reasons for this may be an assumption that the majority of school classes are mono-lingual and mono-cultural, but even in rural areas this may not be the case (Wyse *et al.*, 2011). Even if very few pupils speak additional languages, dialect and register are still part of the linguistic diversity.

Every child, class, school, community and nation has unique contexts for language. National curricula should encourage understanding and analysis of diversity, and should encourage teachers to build upon diversity as a normal daily part of teaching and learning. Rather than viewing languages as 'additional' they should be regarded as part of the linguistic reality that is part of the world we live in. For these reasons the subject title 'language' (as in Scotland, Northern Ireland and Wales) is perhaps the most succinct, encompassing and meaningful title for the subject area rather than the more restrictive use of English. Similarly 'talk' or 'talking' is more accurate and natural, and avoids the unfortunate connotations with formality of the term 'speaking and listening'.

The vital importance of motivating pupils through enjoyment, choice, and even love, is a powerful feature of language curricula. Scotland's inclusion of the statutory requirement to ensure choice, particularly in relation to pupils' writing, is striking and should be replicated elsewhere. The need for pupils to make choices is not only for reasons of empowerment, it is only when choices are made that full understanding is truly demonstrated. The international trend for greater state control of curriculum and pedagogy has resulted in a serious threat to the development of the higher order thinking that comes from self-determination of learning.

The place of the pupil and their voice should be a vital consideration when developing curricula. But so often the pupil's voice and agency can be represented by no more than rhetorical statements in curriculum texts. As you saw in Chapter 5 the place of assessment is so important with regard to the emphases in the curriculum. Pupils' motivation and the nature of the choices they make can and should be facilitated through appropriate assessment strategies. Children have powerful rights under the CRC, something that all nations are legally obliged to take account of when designing curricula. This should at the very least ensure that children are genuinely included in curriculum design over a sufficient timescale, and that their ideas influence decisions at least as much as adult interest groups. One-off consultations about new developments in curricula are insufficient. Facilitating pupils' choices, needs, and interests should be a central concern, not only within language curricula but also within the curriculum as whole.

The commitment to a holistic perspective on reading and writing is another powerful feature of curricula in Northern Ireland, Scotland and Wales. An emphasis on whole texts generally comes first, and word-level understanding, for example of the alphabetic code, is appropriately seen as necessary but limited knowledge to supporting reading and writing. However, in England the trajectory of reform of the 'literacy' and 'English' curricula has shown an increasing dominance of teaching of the alphabetic code, contrary to a balanced consideration of the research evidence, and contrary to curriculum policy in the other three nations of the UK.

Whilst few would now argue that language is not an important feature of early years' and primary teaching and learning, there are still a number of questions that need to be asked. One of the key questions concerns the balance between talk, reading and writing. To answer this question there is a need to separate the curriculum content to be covered from the nature of teacher interaction. It seems to us that most of the debates about oracy and the recent considerations of talk in teaching and learning have more to do with types of interaction than subject content or programmes of study. If national curricula are present, as they are in the UK, then it is appropriate that they should specify the content of the curriculum. This can apply to talk just as it can apply to reading and writing and other subjects in the curriculum. However, there is a need for clear thinking about what the content should be. We would argue that if teachers' practice more routinely encouraged elements such as exploratory talk and dialogic teaching then it may be appropriate to *reduce* the overall content of the programmes of study for talk. This would require renewed thinking about what the content should be and might lead to a greater focus on some of the kinds of language exploration quite rightly advocated by England's Language in the National Curriculum (LINC) project (Carter, 1990) that was underpinned by the kinds of linguistic principles listed earlier in this chapter.

Teacher education/training task

Carry out a survey of the languages used by children in a class you teach. Involve the children as much as possible in the design and implementation of the survey.

Further reading

Crystal, D. (2004). *The Stories of English*. London: Penguin/Allen Lane.
A very enjoyable account of English as a language and its history.
Graves, D.H. (1983). *Writing: Teachers and Children at Work*. Portsmouth, NH: Heinemann Educational.
A compelling account of how to motivate children to write.
Wyse, D. and Jones, R. (forthcoming). *Teaching English, Language and Literacy* (3rd edn). London: Routledge.
A comprehensive and critical account of the different elements of language teaching including those required by national curricula.

References

Alvermann, D. (2008). Why bother theorizing adolescents' online literacies for classroom practice and research? *Journal of Adolescent & Adult Literacy*, 52(1), 8–19.
Andrews, R., Torgerson, C.J., Low, G., McGuinn, N. and Robinson, A. (2006). Teaching argumentative non-fiction writing to 7–14 year olds: a systematic review of the evidence of successful practice. Technical report. *Research Evidence in Education Library*, retrieved 29 January 2007, from http://eppi.ioe.ac.uk/cms/.
Andrews, R., Torgerson, C., Beverton, S., Locke, T., Low, G., Robinson, A. and Zhu, D. (2004). The effect of grammar teaching (syntax) in English on 5 to 16 year olds' accuracy and quality in written composition. *Research Evidence in Education Library*, retrieved 5 February 2007, from http://eppi.ioe.ac.uk/cms/.
Bloodgood, J. (1999). What's in a name? Children's name writing and literacy acquisition. *Reading Research Quarterly*, 34(3), 342–367.
Bolton, E. (2003). Chinese Englishes: from canton jargon to global English. *World Englishes*, 21(2), 181–199.
Bradford, H. and Wyse, D. (2010). Writing in the early years. In D. Wyse, R. Andrews and J. Hoffman (eds), *The International Handbook of English, Language and Literacy Teaching*. London: Routledge, 137–145.

Carter, R. (ed.) (1990). *Knowledge about Language and the Curriculum: The LINC Reader.* London: Hodder & Stoughton.

Chall, J. (1983). *Learning to Read: The Great Debate* (updated edn). New York: McGraw-Hill.

Clarke, M.M. (1976). *Young Fluent Readers: What Can They Teach Us?* London: Heinemann Educational.

Clay, M. (1979). *The Early Detection of Reading Difficulties* (3rd edn). Auckland: Heinemann Education.

Council for the Curriculum Examinations and Assessment (CCEA) (2007). *The Northern Ireland Curriculum Primary.* Belfast: CCEA.

Cox, B. (1991). *Cox on Cox.* London: Hodder & Stoughton.

Crystal, D. (2000). English: which way now? *Spotlight,* April 2000, 54–58.

Crystal, D. (2010). *The Cambridge Encyclopedia of Language* (3rd edn). Cambridge: Cambridge University Press.

Cummins, J. (1979). Linguistic interdependence and the educational development of bilingual children. *Review of Educational Research,* 49(2), 222–251.

D'Agostino, J. and Murphy, J. (2004). A meta-analysis of reading recovery in United States schools. *Educational Evaluation and Policy Analysis,* 26(1), 23–38.

Dahl, K., Scharer, P., Lawson, L. and Grogan, P. (1999). Phonics instruction and student achievement in whole language first-grade classrooms. *Reading Research Quarterly,* 34(3), 312–341.

Department for Children, Education, Lifelong Learning and Skills (2008). *Framework for Children's Learning for 3 to 7-year-olds in Wales.* Cardiff: Welsh Assembly Government.

Department for Education and Employment (DfEE) (1998). *The National Literacy Strategy Framework for Teaching.* Sudbury: DfEE Publications.

Department for Education and Employment (DfEE) and The Qualifications and Curriculum Authority (QCA) (1999). *The National Curriculum. Handbook for Primary Teachers in England. Key Stages 1 and 2.* Norwich: Her Majesty's Stationery Office (HMSO).

Department for Education and Skills (DfES) (2007). The national strategies primary. Primary framework for literacy and mathematics. Retrieved 27 August 2008, from www.standards. dfes.gov.uk/primaryframeworks/.

Durkin, D. (1966). The achievement of pre-school readers: two longitudinal studies. *Reading Research Quarterly,* 1(4), 5–36.

Graham, S. (2006). Strategy instruction and the teaching of writing: a meta-analysis. In S. Graham, C. MacArthur and J. Fitzgerald (eds), *Handbook of Writing Research.* New York: The Guilford Press, 125–136.

Graves, D.H. (1975). An examination of the writing processes of seven year old children. *Research in the Teaching of English,* 9(3), 227–241.

Halliday, M. (2003). Written language, standard language, global language. *World Englishes,* 22(4), 405–418.

Jewitt, C. and Kress, G. (2010). Multimodality, literacy and school English. In D. Wyse, R. Andrews and J. Hoffman (eds), *The Routledge International Handbook of English, Language and Literacy Teaching.* London: Routledge, 342–353.

Juzwik, M., Nystrand, M., Kelly, S. and Sherry, M. (2008). Oral narrative genres as dialogic resources for classroom literature study: a contextualized case study of conversational narrative discussion. *American Educational Research Journal,* 45(4), 1111–1154.

Kovelman, I., Baker, S.A. and Petitto, L. (2008). Bilingual and monolingual brains compared: a functional magnetic resonance imaging investigation of syntactic processing and a possible 'neural signature' of bilingualism. *Journal of Cognitive Neuroscience,* 20(1), 153–169.

Reinking, D. (2010). An outward, inward, and school-ward overview of interactive communication technologies across the literacy landscape. In D. Wyse, R. Andrews and J. Hoffman (eds), *The Routledge International Handbook of English, Language and Literacy Teaching.* London: Routledge, 328–341.

Rosenblatt, L. (1985). Viewpoints: transaction versus interaction: a terminological rescue operation. *Research in the Teaching of English*, 19(1), 96–107.

Scottish Government (2011). Curriculum for excellence, from www.ltscotland.org.uk/ (accessed 1 March 2012).

Simensen, A.M. (2010). English in Scandinavia: a success story. In D. Wyse, R. Andrews and J. Hoffman (eds), *The Routledge International Handbook of English, Language and Literacy Teaching*. Abingdon: Routledge, 472–483.

Smagorinsky, P. (1987). Graves revisited: a look at the methods and conclusions of the New Hampshire study. *Written Communication*, 4(4), 331–342.

Stanovich, K. (1986). Matthew effects in reading: some consequences of individual differences in the acquisition of literacy. *Reading Research Quarterly*, 21(4), 360–407.

Treiman, R., Pennington, B., Shriberg, D. and Boada, R. (2008). Which children benefit from letter names in learning letter sounds? *Cognition*, 106, 1322–1338.

Wigfield, A. and Guthrie, J. (1997). Relations of children's motivation for reading to the amount and breadth of their reading. *Journal of Educational Psychology*, 89(3), 420–432.

Wyse, D. (1988). *Primary Writing*. Buckingham: Open University Press.

Wyse, D. (2001). Grammar. For writing? A critical review of empirical evidence. *British Journal of Educational Studies*, 49(4), 411–427.

Wyse, D. (2006). Pupils' word choices and the teaching of grammar. *Cambridge Journal of Education*, 36(1), 31–47.

Wyse, D. (2007). *How to Help Your Child Read and Write*. London: Pearson Education Limited.

Wyse, D. (2010). Contextualised phonics teaching. In K. Hall, U. Goswami, C. Harrison, S. Ellis and J. Soler (eds), *Interdisciplinary Perspectives on Learning to Read: Culture, Cognition and Pedagogy*. London: Routledge, 130–148.

Wyse, D. (2011). The control of language or the language of control? Primary teachers' knowledge in the context of policy. In S. Ellis and E. McCarthy (eds), *Applied Linguistics and the Primary School*. Cambridge: Cambridge University Press, 21–31.

Wyse, D. and Goswami, U. (2008). Synthetic phonics and the teaching of reading. *British Educational Research Journal*, 34(6), 691–710.

Wyse, D. and Jones, R. (2008). *Teaching English, Language and Literacy* (2nd edn). London: Routledge.

Wyse, D., Andrews, R. and Hoffman, J. (eds) (2010). *The Routledge International Handbook of English, Language, and Literacy Teaching*. London: Routledge.

Wyse, D., Nikolajeva, M., Charlton, E., Cliff Hodges, G., Pointon, P. and Taylor, L. (2011). Place-related identity, texts, and transcultural meanings. *British Educational Research Journal*. doi: 10.1080/01411926.2011.608251.

Yeh, S. (1998). Empowering education: teaching argumentative writing to cultural minority middle-school students. *Research in the Teaching of English*, 33(1), 49–83.

Chapter 8

Critical analysis of Personal and Social Education in UK primary curricula

Ruth Leitch

Society has become increasingly focused on the promotion of children's mental health as an antidote to what is viewed as a rising tide of social and public health issues. In children and young people these are manifest as violence, bullying, underage pregnancy, suicide, or drug and alcohol use. Nationally and internationally schools are identified as one of the priority sites for the promotion of children's emotional health and well-being, and teachers as the most appropriate carriers of knowledge, skills and awareness to address such problems. In each of the four nations of the UK the approach has been to isolate an element within the curricula that aims to address the social and emotional development of children and youth. This element of the curriculum or discrete 'subject area' generally goes under the heading of personal and social education or PSE[1] but has a different nomenclature across England, Northern Ireland, Scotland and Wales.

Development of PSE and the use of terminology

PSE is strongly associated with supporting the development of mental health and well-being in children and young people through timetabled taught 'courses'. Mental health and well-being is defined by the World Health Organisation (2001) as:

> a state of emotional and social well-being in which the individual realizes his or her own abilities, can cope with the normal stresses of life, can work productively, or fruitfully, and is able to make a contribution to his or her community.

In this sense, the core concept of mental health is viewed as foundational to children's and young people's flourishing, for individuals' well-being as well as for the betterment of communities and wider society. It is however very difficult to come to an agreed definition of well-being and, more recently, there has been a somewhat dangerous inclination to reduce it to an approximation for emotional literacy and emotional intelligence (Coleman, 2009). Nevertheless, promoting well-being through PSE is commonly considered integral to fulfilling many schools' universalising mission statements, which proclaim 'to prepare children to their fullest potential, socially, emotionally and academically'. Its inclusion in the curriculum has received political support since the 1970s. Pring (1984) believed that providing social and emotional support can best be achieved through PSE because its inclusion in the curriculum forces us 'to attend to certain features of being a person, which can so easily get lost in the more utilitarian aims of the education system' (p. 15). More recently, MacDonald (2009, p. 5), in his comprehensive review of England's approach to PSE, suggested that 'the prominence of the subject has in fact grown in recent years, particularly with the increased focus on *Every Child Matters* outcomes that were a feature of New Labour education policy, and the duty on schools to promote their pupils' wellbeing'.

PSE is not a term that enjoys international recognition but the concepts are articulated elsewhere, for example in Europe, through such subjects as Civics, Life Skills or Social Education (Lang *et al.*, 1998). Emphases in what constitutes PSE have also tended to vary across different writers as well as across the various policy contexts in the UK. PSE tends to be conceptualised most helpfully in the metaphor of an 'umbrella term' that refers to an amalgam or grouping of areas such as health education, sex education, relationship education, drugs education, social education (civics), moral education, careers and enterprise/financial education. Many of these learning areas can be found in other national curricula but are not likely to be found grouped together under a heading and into a subject area which aims to balance 'personal education' with 'social education' in quite the manner that happens in the UK.

Specific reference to the goals of personal and social education has been around, in various forms, in the UK since the 1970s, in such initiatives as Active Tutorial Work (Baldwin and Wells, 1979) and Life Skills (Hopson and Scally, 1981). It is also associated with the broader development of pastoral care systems and structures in schooling, often referred to as the 'pastoral dimension' (Best, 2000, p. 8). Best (1999) argued that the concern of pastoral care and PSE had been the development and support of the pupil as a person and as a social being through all-round development of the child as a person rather than simply focusing on promoting academic achievement. In this sense, pastoral care is the term usually applied to the ways in which schools respond to social and emotional aspects of development through whole school approaches, such as ethos, care structures, and guidance and child protection policies, alongside more focused elements such as individual tutoring and the planned curricular areas of PSE. Best *et al.* (1980) stated that 'schools up and down the country were searching for a way of backing up their one-to-one pastoral care with a structured curricular approach' (p. 169). PSE and its associated areas were to become this approach enshrined in a school's timetable. Through recent debate, discourse and developments surrounding PSE, there is evidence of a renewed focus on the importance of schools and teachers taking a much more proactive approach to supporting the development of children's health, well-being and personal development through specific curricular initiatives – initiatives that are preventive, and that promote positive mental health by emphasising agency and resilience in children through paying attention to the affective dimensions of children's experience.

PSE aims to promote an underpinning model that connects emotion and reason in weighing up children and young people's informed life choices and decision-making. If emotion is part of thinking and decision-making processes then it is argued that the development of emotional intelligence is central to achieving better life choices. This underlying assumption and its consequences played out through PSE as a taught subject is not without its critics. Thus, Craig (2007) protests against a diminished view of the child whereby pupils are viewed as lacking in capacity to deal with emotions and where, through curriculum subjects like PSE, teachers are charged to make good this deficit. Moreover, Ecclestone and Hayes (2009) decry what they see as a shift to a 'therapeutic culture' in schooling in which interventions such as PSE are based on the inherent idea that there are emotional aspects of learning and attending to these will increase learning. Some forms of PSE programmes or class activities they consider go well beyond this and simply promote the discourse and practices of psychotherapy in schools by focusing unnecessarily on the 'language of feelings, introspection, fragility and vulnerability' rather than self-efficacy (Craig, 2007, p. 15). Sarup (1982), too, suggests that the growth of these areas (PSE/pastoral care) represent an increasing intervention by the state, and what may appear as compassionate care for the individual child is really an attempt to socialize the 'deviant'. Such critics thus caution about the dangers of PSE masquerading as social control.

Key questions for reflection

Do you think schools and teachers should have a central role in the promotion of children's social and emotional well-being, or do you think this is simply a form of social control through schooling?

Details of UK regional approaches to the structure and delivery of PSE

Although regularly referred to in national curriculum policies for England, Northern Ireland (NI), Scotland and Wales until recently, PSE has not had a statutory requirement for delivery through the curriculum. Introducing PSE as a legal requirement remains a hotly debated issue in England where it has been resisted, while in other regions, such as NI, it is a statutory obligation. Despite these formal status differences in PSE as a discrete curriculum subject area, nevertheless, there is some agreement across the UK in relation to the aims of PSE. There is however less agreement on what should constitute the most significant elements of PSE in the various jurisdictions, demonstrated in an overall lack of coherence across the four nations. Some of these tensions and differences are reflected in the miscellany of terminology associated with PSE as well as manifesting somewhat differently in content, pedagogy and approaches to assessment. Thus, at primary level we have personal social health and economic education (PSHE) in England; personal development and mutual understanding (PDMU) in Northern Ireland; personal and social development (PSD) in Scotland, and personal and social education (PSE) in Wales. In order to draw comparisons across the UK, regional variations in policy and practices of PSE in the curriculum will now be addressed under the relevant country headings.

England

In England, personal social and health and economic education (PSHE) has been part of the national curriculum for schools in England since 2000. As a subject area concerned with helping children and young people develop fully as individuals and as members of families and social and economic communities, it extends and supports existing policy strategies such as National Healthy Schools (1999), Every Child Matters (2003) and is supported by the Children Act (2004). PSHE in England is most closely aligned with health education but also, at Key Stages 1 and 2, coexists with citizenship in a non-statutory framework. There are also associations with financial awareness, competence and careers education that have crept in more visibly at secondary level. However, unlike other traditional subjects, PSHE has had no statutory programme. This means that the content to be taught in PSHE has been a matter for 'guidance rather than prescription' (Haydon, 2010, p. 504) leaving to schools and teachers the final decisions about what and how this area of the curriculum is to be taught.

In recent years PSHE in the curriculum has had a higher profile in public debate and there have been arguments that PSHE should indeed have a statutory programme of study. The MacDonald Review (2009) determined that children and young people of all ages value learning about personal and social development and thus PSHE ought to be recognised more fully. The recommendations were that all children and young people should have a statutory entitlement to the common core of knowledge, skills and understanding found within the PSHE domain. Subsequently the Children, Schools and Families (CSF) Bill was to provide the legislative framework for giving PSHE statutory status. However with a change of government in 2010 and spurred on by seemingly contentious proposals for compulsory sex education for children as young as five, all the momentum leading towards a statutory basis for PSHE has ceased and has led to the launch of yet another review of this curricular area by the Coalition government.

Key questions for reflection

What do you think is the appropriate age of the child to experience lessons on sex and relationship education?

Some of the concerns raised by the proposed introduction of compulsory PSHE in England (and Wales) relate to the statutory inclusion of sex education. This has resulted in a number of pressure groups, especially family campaigners, fearing that sex education with the 'impressionistic' young is unacceptable and too much information too early will be detrimental and may lead to sexual precociousness. Consequently, the teaching of sex education will remain optional in primary schools in England (and Wales) for the time being.

In the light of concerns about teachers' confidence to teach this area, the Social and Emotional Aspects of Learning (SEAL) resource was initiated, piloted and promoted across primary schools[2] to help teachers develop social and emotional skills in children.[3] Basing its rationale on national and international research evidence from the field that links educational achievement to a preventative approach to mental health (Elias et al., 1997; Wells et al., 2003) and arguments from neuroscience and emotional intelligence, SEAL has been promoted as providing a developmentally progressive and themed approach to the explicit teaching of social and emotional skills through a spiral curriculum. What this means is that pupils are to revisit and build on PSE content at the different levels of development and at different levels of subject matter and skills. The key underpinning principles to the SEAL approach are:

- using a whole-school approach to create the climate and conditions that implicitly promote the skills and allow them to be practised and consolidated;
- providing direct and focused learning opportunities for whole classes (during tutor time, across the curriculum and outside formal lessons) and as part of focus group work;
- using learning and teaching approaches that support pupils to learn social and emotional skills and consolidate those already learned; and
- facilitating continuing professional development for the whole staff of a school.

(Michel and Noble, 2007, p. 232)

Arguably, then, what is distinctive about SEAL materials has been the determination to promote social and emotional development as coherent and seamlessly integrated into the work of schools rather than having to be incorporated as an additional area. Making the core learning elements of SEAL (emotional and cognitive skills) align with the 11 aspects of learning that underpinned England's Primary National Strategy's core professional development resources for schools was central to this. There has also been a determination to integrate Assessment for Learning (AfL) principles into materials. The introduction of SEAL as a means for promoting the goals of PSE in the curriculum was subject to a number of evaluations (e.g. Humphrey *et al.*, 2009) which will be reviewed below. Developments of PSE in England (and Wales) however have been contentious and considered by some as fundamentally flawed. Thus, as a counterpoint, Craig (2007, p. 11) argues that SEAL, as a taught approach to social and emotional skills, is essentially 'a short cut, or a band-aid, when what is required is a range of much deeper-seated changes'.

Northern Ireland (NI)

The implementation of the Revised NI Primary Curriculum secured holistic development as a basic entitlement of all learners and placed personal development at the fore of education (CCEA, 2007). PSE was, until 2003, part of the informal curriculum in NI when it became a statutory requirement. It is now under the heading of personal development and mutual understanding (PDMU). PDMU is now one of six discrete learning areas,[4] which focuses on 'children's emotional development, health and safety, relationships with others and development of moral thinking, values and actions' (CCEA, 2007, p. 3). Developing curriculum content and related outcomes for PDMU in NI was viewed at the time of its inception as complementary to the Every Child Matters Agenda in England (Department for Education and Skills, 2004) in terms of: safeguarding the welfare of pupils; promoting health and emotional well-being; and facilitating pupils' well-being by encouraging them to be happy and fulfil their potential in life and work. Since then, there has been a shift away from using the language of Every Child Matters but the ethos of supporting children and young people to stay safe, be healthy, make a positive contribution, and achieve emotional well-being has been retained in PDMU in NI.

According to the Council for Curriculum Examination and Assessment (CCEA) in NI, the effective implementation of the PDMU curriculum in primary schools emphasises variously the development of pupils' empowerment, interdependence, participation, responsible choices, resiliency and transferable skills.

At the foundation stage and Key Stages 1 and 2 in primary education, there are two main but interconnected strands: personal understanding and health and mutual understanding in the local and wider community. The former strand carries many of the learning intentions familiar to PSE curricula elsewhere in England and Wales, with reference to developing self-esteem and confidence, understanding and managing emotions and strategies and skills for children keeping themselves healthy and safe, all of which are intended to remove barriers and reinforce positive attitudes to learning and achievement. Mutual understanding does reflect the links between personal and the social development but with a particular twist which takes cognisance of the current social and political context of Northern Ireland as it emerges post-conflict. The two strands have core areas of development:

Personal understanding and health:

- developing pupil's self-esteem and self-confidence;
- their own and others' feelings and emotions and how their actions affect others;
- positive attitudes to learning and achievement;
- strategies and skills for keeping themselves healthy and safe.

Mutual understanding in the local and wider community:

- initiating and developing mutually satisfying relationships;
- responsibility and respect, honesty and fairness;
- constructive approaches to conflict;
- similarities and differences between people;
- developing themselves as members of a community.

Whilst PDMU is the main curricular area through which health education is taught, it is embedded in the strands rather than identified and taught explicitly. On the other hand, relationships and sexuality education (RSE) is a legal requirement in Northern Ireland and is taught as part of the Science curriculum as well as within PDMU. Each school, as part of the development of its RSE policy, must ensure that its curriculum content and practices are compatible with the overall ethos and values of the school and is based on the rights of the child as detailed in the Children (Northern Ireland) Order, 1995. Consultation with governors, parents and staff (and feedback from children) in the development of policy is recommended as part of the preparation and planning (DENI, 2001). Recognising that RSE can be a sensitive and often contentious area in the curriculum, parents retain the right to withdraw their child and schools are to emphasise positive aspects of relationships and sexuality. However official guidance suggests that 'teachers should not avoid discussion of sensitive issues such as contraception, abortion,

HIV/AIDS and other sexually transmitted diseases, homosexuality and pornography' tailored in a developmentally appropriate manner (DENI Circular, 2001–15).

Although not long embedded in the Northern Ireland primary curriculum, research by Long and McPolin (2010) investigated almost 200 primary (P1 and P5) teachers' views on the formal introduction of PDMU during 2007–2008. What they determined was a commitment to the promotion of PDMU by the majority of primary school principals (70 per cent) evidenced through integration in their school development plans and being regularly timetabled. Teachers felt most confident and experienced in delivering the theme 'Feelings and Emotions' yet reported feeling least confident about delivering the theme 'Relationships' due to the potentially sensitive nature of this area. Findings also suggested that PDMU is seen as extending beyond classrooms acting as a catalyst for the development of partnerships between schools, health professionals, parents and community groups.

Scotland

Personal and Social Development (PSD) is at the heart of Scotland's A Curriculum for Excellence. In primary schools, however, PSD is closely allied to a much broader whole-school approach to the pastoral care of its pupils and, in its expression through the curriculum has reflected a strong health and well-being agenda. The discourse surrounding PSD in Scotland, as with the other four nations, speaks of developing children's personality, talents, mental and physical abilities to their fullest potential but does so by foregrounding concerns for inclusion and pupil voice. Until recently, there seems to have been little in the way of a consistent or coherent learning programme underpinning the teaching of PSD in Scottish primary classrooms. During 2000–2006, HMI evaluations found that, in addition to cross-curricular approaches, which link learning and teaching in PSD, formally and informally with learning in other curriculum areas, many primary schools were addressing PSD by drawing on a range of progressive, often commercially-produced taught programmes, including Circle Time (Mosley, 2006) which rather than promoting specific content emphasises opportunities for supportive discussion of issues of interest or concern to pupils. Approaches such as these have integrated the teaching of PSD with health education and sometimes with philosophy or study skills and more recently with structured programmes in citizenship and enterprise education (HMI, 2007).

Currently there is no legal requirement for Scottish schools to teach sex education, although all schools are encouraged to provide Sexuality and Relationship Education (SRE) within their programme for personal, social and health education or religious and moral education. The emphasis is seen to be on helping young people develop sound lifestyle choices and healthy living within a framework of values rather than providing discrete inputs on aspects of RSE.

There is little independent research on the effectiveness of PSD initiatives in Scotland. There have however been regular published evaluations by the HM Inspectors (2004, 2007) which suggest that almost all primary schools give high priority to PSD, seeing it as a foundation for all other learning and as a way of creating an 'an ethos of achievement'. A plethora of different programmes have been identified covering health education, citizenship, thinking skills, study skills, education for work and enterprise/enterprise in education, career education, sustainable development, anti-bullying and anti-drugs but raise concerns about coherence and progression and the blurring of subject boundaries.

Wales

In Wales, Personal and Social Education is referred to currently as PSE and is part of the wider vision of a curriculum for Wales. Wales has been distinctive within the four nations of the UK in the way in which it has adopted a children's rights' perspective[5] as the basis for its policy-making and implementation, and specifically in relation to education and health. Under the United Nations Convention on the Rights of the Child (UNCRC) and the Welsh Assembly Government's overarching strategy document 'Rights to Action', all children and young people must be provided with an education which develops their personality and talents to the full.

PSE has been a compulsory element in both primary and secondary schools since 2003 (Welsh Assembly Government) as part of its revised curriculum. From autumn 2008, however, there has been a new, more flexibly structured curriculum of PSE for Foundation stage (ages three to seven) which is to be built upon subsequently through a separate framework for 7–19 year olds. The latter focuses on health and emotional well-being and encompasses Sexuality and Relationship Education (SRE) and careers and world of work for those over the age of 11 (Department for Children, Education, Lifelong Learning and Skills (DCELLS), 2008).

In relation to primary education, guidelines within the statutory framework for the Foundation phase refer to 'personal development' and 'social development' separately. Personal development in the framework encompasses the promotion of children's awareness of themselves and the development of their self-help skills. These tie quite specifically to a developmental stages approach to children's growth and development, where learning outcomes relate to progress in what are generally acknowledged to be discrete stage-appropriate developmental tasks associated with such learning areas as body awareness, self-help and independence. Social development, on the other hand, encompasses social interactions and relationships with their peers and adults. As in England, primary schools must have a policy of PSE which makes reference to sex and relationships education (SRE) or at least sets out why this aspect is not included. SRE in Wales is viewed as part of learning about 'healthy relationships' and any teaching is required to be placed within a clear framework of values and an awareness of the law on sexual behaviour but at present is non-statutory.

Wales also draws on the SEAL initiative but, essentially, it is the responsibility of primary schools in Wales to plan and deliver a broad, balanced programme of PSE in order to meet the specific needs of learners. However, cognisant of the need to support teachers in this curricular area, DCELLS has developed a bilingual PSE guidance website to provide specific resources and guidance (www.wales.gov.uk/personalandsocial education) which may be incorporated to promote PSE in the classroom.

Pedagogy and PSE

Haydon (2005, p. 10) refers to the scope of PSE curricular topics as 'vacuously broad' and 'sometimes frustratingly specific in giving a list without an underlying rationale'. The breadth of PSE content adds significantly to the complex issues for teachers regarding decisions about what is the most effective pedagogical approach to take when delivering it in classrooms. From a review of the UK contexts, classroom curriculum delivery methods for PSE can vary substantially. In the absence of a distinct discipline focus and without an agreed or specified body of knowledge to transmit, PSE is viewed largely as process-oriented. Process-orientation requires much greater reliance on teacher facilitation and pedagogical skills to further children's learning as opposed to the straightforward transmission of fact or knowledge. When this process works well and when the conditions are right, this can lead to an excellent learning experience, providing teachers with one of the most creative opportunities to engage with their pupils' learning in the personal and social aspects of modern life that are potentially of immediate interest and long-term importance. However, when it is in the hands of those teachers who are inexperienced, untrained, sceptical or simply fearful, or conducted in an ethos that is not conducive, it can be a very negative learning opportunity for all involved.

In the context of classroom curriculum, delivery methods can vary substantially but frequently rely on the use of small group work. Methods range from ideas generation, games, self-reflection, debate, role-play, co-operative learning, arts-based approaches to teaching and learning, for example, through collage, drawing, simulations and storytelling. Teachers in this area often feel poorly equipped or reluctant to get engaged in the core personal and affective elements of the PSE curriculum using such methods. A central contributory factor is the relative lack of preparation and training. Unlike other traditional subject areas, such as Maths, English, Geography, etc., there is little in the way of subject-specific training for PSE in initial teacher education. An assumption persists that simply by being a good teacher of the conventional subjects, the skills required for PSE should transfer. Given the range of potential content and the focus on knowledge, skills and self-awareness, the logic of this does not readily follow. For example, Oulton *et al.* (2004) found that secondary teachers did not feel adequately prepared to teach controversial issues. Crow (2008) also reinforces the importance of teachers' own lack of confidence in the complex learning tasks involved in PSE. He proposes that PSE is no less a specialism than other subjects but it is never accorded the same parity and teachers are insufficiently supported in the cultivation and development of their expertise in this area.

Notwithstanding this, the Standards for Newly Qualified Teacher Standards (QTS – Training and Development Agency, 2011) in England require that all teachers have some understanding of PSHE education and the legislation that underpins this. The Standards state that: 'All trainees are expected to be familiar with the National Curriculum guidance on personal, social, health and economic education (PSHEE) relevant to the age ranges they are training to teach' (QTS, 15).[6] However being aware of the curriculum content does little to guarantee competent, confident approaches to facilitation and the effective handling of controversial issues. In the absence of initial and progressive in-service training, what tends to happen is a fall-back position, where teachers seek the security of pre-packaged approaches rather than work to improve their own professional style and practice. To illustrate this, when CCEA in NI produced a PDMU resource for each year group in the Living Learning Together series, 95 per cent of the total sample reported that they had used this resource in the academic year 2007/2008 with over 90 per cent of respondents reviewing it in positive terms.

The lacuna in official support and training is one of the reasons that packages such as SEAL and Circle Time have had such significant impact. SEAL, in England and Wales, like most approaches to PSE, argues for a process-oriented approach which emphasises the teacher as 'facilitator' of small group work with children. Humphrey *et al.*'s (2009) research in England found that the quality of delivery was related to the skills and experience of the teacher, some of which entailed setting achievable targets for children, providing constant reinforcement and opportunities for pupils to verbalise their emotional experiences. Pre-dating SEAL, and still popular in the UK, the approach most often linked to PSE and the development of self-esteem in primary schools is Circle Time (Mosley, 1993, 2006). Teachers' qualitative feedback on these approaches also reveals that, in general, they recognise the benefits of using experiential methodologies rather than information transmission in order to create effective PSE classroom experiences.

Self-esteem of course is a notoriously slippery psychological construct. Notwithstanding this, Circle Time methodology is based on the assumptions that the 'self' is a social construction and that self-esteem can be enhanced by addressing both personal concerns and progressively more controversial issues within a safe social and interpersonal climate created in the classroom. Described simply, a teacher sits in a circle with the class of children, together creating a climate of safety through a negotiation of rules, and a significant element of the methodology is based on all children having equal opportunity to speak and be listened to. Despite its popularity in primary schools in each of the four nations there has been little research evidence to evaluate its effectiveness in promoting children's self-esteem. Miller and Moran (2007), however, undertook a systematic evaluation in Scottish primary schools and found that while Circle Time was more likely to help children develop a sense of self-worth (based on self-report), other efficacy approaches focusing on the achievement of performance goals also improved children's self-competence. Two issues emerge from this consideration: one is that primary school teachers have valued the resource and training available for Circle Time which has demystified small group processes. Second, arising from the study, is the implication that teachers and educators need further opportunities to deconstruct such notions as self-esteem (amongst other constructs such as well-being) and consider more deeply what exactly they are trying to achieve when the enhancement of pupils' self-esteem is their goal.

Both of these approaches (SEAL and Circle Time) appear to be complementary, as Formby (2011) identified that aspects of PSHE in England were most likely to be taught within SEAL lessons, using Circle Time teaching approaches. And, in their NI study, Long and McPolin (2010) found that the majority of teachers in both Year One and Year Five cited Circle Time as being their main resource with a significant number also citing role-play, drama, music and stories. These arts-based approaches, it seems, allow for imaginative means to develop the affective dimension inherent in PSE. On the other hand, the argument remains that there is a danger in 'introducing topics to do with emotions into the curriculum, partly because teachers are not trained to deal with such materials' (Coleman, 2009, p. 290).

PSE delivered effectively involves teachers in a very skilful approach to pedagogy that facilitates pupils' awareness, skills and knowledge across a broad range of topics and, in the absence of proper support and training, its credibility is too readily under threat. The most negative consequences of this leads to it being viewed as a low status subject (by teachers, parents and pupils), easily dismissed at the margins of the timetable, in a world where there is the potential for education to be viewed instrumentally and where curriculum areas compete for time and resources.

Research evidence on impact of PSE

There is some serious debate, in political as well as educational fora, on the extent to which PSE can make a significant impact on the improvement of children's socio-emotional behaviour and well-being. Back as far as 1966, Carey argued that such curricular programmes did not have the capacity to undo the structural forces that engendered the underlying issues such as poverty and deprivation that are associated with the development of children's mental health and well-being issues in the first place.

Research about whether or not PSE programmes in schools are able to enhance well-being and deliver their intended learning outcomes is fraught with complexity. At the moment there is no robust evidence base. Amongst other things, there is no shared agreement about definitions and thus how to measure outcomes empirically, many of which are subjective, such as emotional well-being, for example.

Compounding this and arising from the above discussions is that context and the range of PSE programmes on offer vary enormously as do the associated delivery processes – some schools/teachers emphasise increasing pupil self-awareness, some emphasise pupils being able to apply good information while still others focus on enhancing their social and emotional coping skills. So there is a question of what kind of outcome can and should be measured in order to demonstrate any credible evidence of impact and how could any systematic study take satisfactory account of the huge complexity of variables?

Until recently, in the UK, there has been relatively little systematic or longitudinal research into the effectiveness and success of specific educational interventions related to the goals of PSE on children and young peoples' lives (Coleman, 2009; DCSF, 2009). Perhaps in recognition of the complexity of the field, empirical research on PSE has, rather, tended to be indirect, and undertaken as part of major projects on the effects of preventive programmes such as, for example, diet, smoking, sexual behaviours, alcohol use and drugs (Chamberlain *et al.*, 2010). Where data are available about the impact on young people, more often than not, such studies try to capture evidence through self-report on behavioural patterns and attitudes to issues that affect them, all of which can be open to charges of unreliability (Coleman, 2009).

Evidence has only just started to accumulate about the wider impact of PSE (Shucksmith and Spratt, 2002). Thus, research has more recently turned to analysing what are the characteristics that make for effective interventions in schools and classrooms. In 2003, Wells *et al.* carried out a systematic review of the impact of programmes on mental health promotion and found that evidence of effectiveness was obtained for interventions (mostly in the United States) that 'adopted a whole-school approach, were implemented continuously for more than a year, and were aimed at the promotion of mental health as opposed to the prevention of mental illness' (p. 197).

Despite all the identified challenges to research in this area, Hallam (2009), in her national evaluation of the SEAL initiative in England, found that relationships between teachers and pupils were significant in the delivery of PSE, reporting that children were identified as being 'better and calmer' (p. 321) as a result. By contrast Craig (2007) warns that SEAL may be a 'waste of time and resources [and] in fact . . . undermine young people's wellbeing' (p. 2).

Lendrum *et al.* (2009) went on to evaluate SEAL through detailed case studies in five lead practice primary schools. Their specific focus was to identify models of effective practice in PSE through in-depth study of the pedagogical processes observed in PSE classrooms. Examining small group processes, they discerned that the most common and effective format

> begins with a welcome and check-in, followed by warm-up activities, reminder of group aims and rules, review of the previous week and plan for current session, a core activity, review and reflection, plans for the coming week and finally a relaxation activity.
>
> (p. 235)

Likewise, Parton and Manby (2009) reported on a small but systematic study on the impact of using regular small groupwork in primary schools in the north of England. What they determined was that, although there were indeed significant but statistically small improvements in children's behaviours, this was not the case for the most disruptive children. From their analysis, these children really required more specialist and sustained support and interventions to improve their social skills. This tends to indicate that PSE outcomes were not positive for everyone and PSE, it seems, was not a panacea.

Key questions for reflection

Do you think PSE is appropriate for all children? If not, what other educational and behavioural support might need to be offered?

Research specifically focusing on the impact of PSE is largely missing in Scotland and Wales outside formal statutory inspections, although a number of these have thrown up some robust observations about 'what works'. Based on evidence arising from the national inspection programme of primary schools, HM Inspectorate (2007) was able to compare indicators of progress in PSD in Scotland from 2002 to that which was observed in 2006, documenting quite specific improvements as well as challenges involved in enabling Scottish pupils to develop life skills for use beyond their primary classrooms.

Two independent research studies in Northern Ireland tend to reinforce the trends in effectiveness identified in England. Leitch *et al.* (2005), exploring best practice models for PSE in the NI context, found that where a teacher places a high premium on the process of the lesson, where they have built strong relationships with the class, were able to negotiate curricular content and respond to pupils' needs in the 'live moment', all of these contributed to effective learning experiences for slightly older pupils undertaking PSE. Later, Long and McPolin (2010) surveyed just under 200 primary 1 and primary 5 classroom teachers and found that despite the constraints of time, training and teacher confidence, the PDMU curriculum in NI was viewed as beneficial although the content still tended to be adult-led and not always consistent with ideas of pupil consultation. They went on to build a profile of PDMU where one-third of teachers only identified that PDMU had a regular timetable slot, with a minority indicating that they were using whole-school approaches including the establishment of school councils, healthy schools initiatives and emotional literacy programmes to promote personal and social education with health education in its widest sense.

Summary and implications for practice

This chapter has examined the various ways in which PSE has been conceptualised in each of the four nations of the UK and identified the differing ways in which certain aspects of PSE have been foregrounded in the structure and content of the curriculum and how in the final analysis it still remains at the mercy of political whim and policy flux. It has explored how important it is for practitioners to understand and adopt a critical perspective on the underlying intentions and values associated with PSE and its role in promoting children's well-being as opposed to engendering conformity and promoting social control. The various synergies and dissonances between approaches to PSE across the differing contexts of the UK have resulted in a miscellany of pedagogical and assessment practices and teachers require more opportunities for training in this area right from initial teacher education. Seasoned practitioners also need to be encouraged to be continually reflective not only about their approaches to facilitating this complex area but also on how they might develop their practice with a view to ongoing improvement and sharing of good practice. Any improvement should specifically address how teachers might consult with pupils more fully on selecting content, approaches to teaching and learning and any assessment involved, thus 'enshrining a learning voice'. The overall discussion points have raised some of the critique and polemic stimulated by the inclusion of the affective element in the curriculum and concludes by encouraging policy-makers, practitioners and researchers to collaborate on developing robust, relevant and creative evaluation measures of the impact of PSE on children's personal and social development for future direction.

Suggested tasks

Select a topic that might be included in a PSE curriculum (e.g. developing empathy; handling anger in self and other). In a small group develop what you consider might be an appropriate set of learning outcomes for a specific primary class. Then design a process-oriented lesson. What style and approach might you need to adopt to ensure that the children developed knowledge, skills and awareness in relation to the issue? How would you know? How might you plan for learning progression? How would you ensure safety in the learning group?

Take the opportunity to try out the lesson and any resources developed with another group of student teachers to obtain feedback.

Further reading

Ecclestone, K. and Hayes, D. (2008) *The Dangerous Rise of Therapeutic Education*. London: Routledge.
This reading provides an interesting critique of the rise of 'therapeutic education' in schooling.
Formby, E. (2011) 'It's better to learn about your health and things that are going to happen to you than learning things that you just do at school': findings from a mapping study of PSHE education in primary schools in England. *Pastoral Care in Education*, 29 (3), pp. 161–173.
Based on a mapping study of schools in England, this article raises issues about blurred boundaries between PSHE and Social and Emotional Aspects of Learning (SEAL) and/or pastoral care within schools more widely.
Haydon, G. (2010) Personal and social education. In Bailey, R., Barrow, R., Carr, D. and McCarthy, C. (eds) *The International Handbook of Philosophy of Education*. London: Sage, pp. 503–515. This chapter provides a contemporary examination of some of the key issues facing teachers of PSE in today's classrooms.
Pring, R. (1984) *Personal and Social Education in the Curriculum*. London: Hodder & Stoughton.
This seminal book outlines the importance in the curriculum of personal and social development and how it might be translated into curriculum terms. It presents the philosophical underpinnings of PSE and also provides practical suggestions for teachers in the classroom.

Notes

1   Within this chapter, the term Personal and Social Education (PSE) is used to refer generically to this area of the curriculum. Specific local terms are used when discussing how PSE is manifested within each of the four nations of the UK.
2   SEAL was designed for universal provision by DCSF, and it is planned that by the year 2011 all children and young people in state schools in England (19,000 primary schools and 3,700 secondary schools) will have opportunities to experience SEAL. A phased national implementation in secondary schools started in September 2007 following a pilot project (Michel and Noble, 2009).
3   The Department for Children, Schools and Families (DCSF) supported the development of SEAL. DCSF existed between 2007 and 2010, and was responsible for issues affecting children and young people in England up to the age of 19. The DCSF was replaced by the Department of Education after the change of government in 2010.

4   The six discrete learning areas in the NI revised curriculum include language and literacy; mathematics and numeracy; the world around us; the arts; physical development and movement and personal development and mutual understanding.
5   As defined by the United Nations Convention on the Rights of the Child (UNCRC). See Chapter 3 for the seven core aims for children and young people that arise from this commitment.
6   In March 2011, the Coalition government launched the Independent Review of Teachers' Standards in England, to be chaired by Sally Coates, the outcome of which may alter the emphasis of standards associated with teachers' knowledge and understanding for PSE.

References

Baldwin, J. and Wells, H. (1979) *Active Tutorial Work. Book 1 [The First Year]*. Oxford: Blackwell, Lancashire County Council.

Best, R. (1999) The impact of a decade of education on pastoral care and personal development. A survey of teachers' perceptions. *Pastoral Care in Education*, 17 (2), pp. 3–13.

Best, R. (2000) Empathy, experience and SMSC (spiritual moral social and cultural). *Pastoral Care in Education*, 22 (1), pp. 1–18.

Best, R., Jarvis, C. and Ribbins, P. (eds) (1980) *Perspectives on Pastoral Care*. London: Heinemann Organisation in Schools Series.

CCEA (2007) *Personal Development and Mutual Understanding: Key Stages 1 & 2, Guidance*. Northern Ireland Curriculum, CCEA, www.nicurriculum.org.uk/docs/personal_development/training/PD-Guidance.pdf (accessed September 2011).

Chamberlain, T., George, N., Golden, S., Walker, F. and Benton, T. (2010) Tellus4 national report (DCSF Research Report 218). London: DCSF.

Coleman, J. (2009) Well-being in schools: empirical measure, or politician's dream? *Oxford Review of Education*, 35 (3), pp. 281–292.

Craig, C. (2007) The potential dangers of a systematic, explicit approach to teaching social and emotional skills (SEAL): an overview and summary of the arguments. Centre for Confidence and Well-being, www.centreforconfidence.co.uk/docs/SEALsummary.pdf (accessed October 2011).

Crow, F. (2008) Learning for well-being: personal, social and health education and a changing curriculum. *Pastoral Care in Education*, 26 (1), pp. 43–51.

Department for Children, Education, Lifelong Learning and Skills (Yr Adran Plant, Addysg, Dysgu Gydol Oes a Sgiliau) (2008) Personal and social education and careers and the world of work in the basic curriculum. Welsh Assembly Government Circular No: 24/2008 Replaces Circular No: 13/03, http://wales.gov.uk/pubs/circulars/2008/circular24/eng.pdf?lang=en (accessed October 2010).

Department for Children, Schools and Families (DCSF) (2009) Personal, Social, Health and Economic (PSHE) education: research evidence note. London: Analysis and Research Division, Schools Research Team.

Department of Education for Northern Ireland (DENI) (2001) Guidance for primary schools: relationships and sexuality education (RSE) circular 2001/15.

Department for Education and Skills (2004) Every child matters: change for children, November. DfES/1081/2004, www.education.gov.uk/publications/standard/publicationdetail/page1/DfES/1081/2004 (accessed September 2011).

Ecclestone, K. and Hayes, D. (2009) *The Dangerous Rise of Therapeutic Education*. London: Routledge.

Elias, M., Zins, J. and Weissberg, R. (1997) *Promoting Social and Emotional Learning: Guidelines for Educators*. Illinois: ASCD.

Formby, E. (2011) 'It's better to learn about your health and things that are going to happen to you than learning things that you just do at school': findings from a mapping study of PSHE education in primary schools in England. *Pastoral Care in Education*, 29 (3), pp. 161–173.

Hallam, S. (2009) An evaluation of the Social and Emotional Aspects of Learning (SEAL) programme: promoting positive behaviour, effective learning and well-being in primary schools. *Oxford Review of Education*, 35 (3), pp. 313–330.

Haydon, G. (2005) Impact 10: the importance of PSHE: a philosophical and policy perspective on personal, social and health education. London: Philosophy of Education Society of Great Britain.

Haydon, G. (2010) Personal and social education. In Bailey, R., Barrow, R., Carr, D. and McCarthy, C. (eds) *The International Handbook of Philosophy of Education*. London: Sage, pp. 503–515.

Hopson, B. and Scally, M. (1981) *Lifeskills Teaching*. Maidenhead: McGraw-Hill.

HM Inspectorate for Education (Scotland) (2004) Personal support for pupils in Scottish Schools: a report, www.hmie.gov.uk/documents/publication/pspss-02.html (accessed October 2010).

HM Inspectorate for Education (Scotland) (2007) Ready for life: education for personal and social development in primary schools, www.hmie.gov.uk/documents/publication/Ready%20for%20Life%20_PSD_%2028.03.07.pdf (accessed October 2010).

Humphrey, N., Lendrum, A., Wiglesworth, M. and Kalambouka, A. (2009) Implementation of primary Social and Emotional Aspects of Learning small group work: a qualitative study. *Pastoral Care in Education*, 27 (3), pp. 219–239.

Lang, P., Katz, Y. and Menezes, I. (eds) (1998) *European Affective Education*. London: Cassell.

Leitch, R., Mitchell, S. and Kilpatrick, R. (2005) A study into current practice and potential models for the effective teaching of personal development at key stage 3 in the Northern Ireland curriculum, Department of Education (NI) Briefing, No. 38, www.deni.gov.uk/researchreport38_2005.pdf (accessed September 2011).

Lendrum, A., Humphrey, N., Kalambouka, A. and Wigelsworth, M. (2009) Implementing primary Social and Emotional Aspects of Learning (SEAL) small group interventions: recommendations for practitioners. *Emotional and Behavioural Difficulties*, 14 (3), pp. 229–238.

Living Learning Together: Personal Development and Mutual Understanding, www.nicurriculum.org.uk/docs/key_stages_1_and_2/areas_of_learning/pdmu/livinglearningtogether/year7/yr7_intro.pdf (accessed November 2011).

Long, L. and McPolin, B. (2010) Personal and civic education in the Northern Ireland primary curriculum: teachers' perspectives. *Pastoral Care in Education*, 28 (2), pp. 109–129.

MacDonald, A. (2009) Independent review of the proposal to make PSHE education statutory, Department for Children, Schools and Families, http://publications.dcsf.gov.ukdefault.aspxPageFunction=productdetails&PageMode=publications&ProductId=DCSF-00495–2009 (accessed October 2010).

Michel, D. and Noble, C. 2007. Executive summary. United Kingdom (England): the framework and the process – how social and emotional aspects of learning (SEAL) addresses the mental well-being of adolescents through the context of healthy schools.

Miller, D. and Moran, T. (2007) Theory and practice in self-esteem enhancement: circle-time and efficacy-based approaches – a controlled evaluation. *Teachers and Teaching: Theory and Practice*, 13 (6), pp. 601–615.

Mosley, J. (1993) Turn your school round LDA Wisbech, Cambridgeshire.

Mosley, J. (2006) *Step-by-Step Guide to Circle Time for SEAL*. Trowbridge: Positive Press Ltd.

Newly Qualified Teacher Standards (QTS) by the Teacher Development Agency (TDA) (2011), www.hmie.gov.uk/documents/publication/pspss-02.html (accessed October 2011).

Oulton, C., Day, V., Dillon, J. and Grace, M. (2004) Controversial issues – teacher's attitudes and practices in the context of citizenship education. *Oxford Review of Education*, 30 (4), pp. 389–507.

Parton, C. and Manby, M. (2009) The contribution of group work programmes to early intervention and improving children's emotional well-being. *Pastoral Care in Education*, 27 (1), pp. 5–19.

Pring, R. (1984) *Personal and Social Education in the Curriculum*. London: Hodder & Stoughton.

Sarup, M. (1982) *Education, State and Crisis*. London: Routledge and Kegan Paul.

Shucksmith, J. and Spratt, J. (2002) HEBS, young people and health initiative: young people's self identified health needs, University of Aberdeen, May 2002, p. 25, www.healthscotland. com/uploads/documents/RE06220012002Final.pdf (accessed October 2010).

Wells, J., Barlow, J. and Stewart-Brown, S. (2003) *A Systematic Review of Universal Approaches to Mental Health Promotion in Schools*. Oxford: University of Oxford Institute of Health Sciences.

Welsh Assembly Government 'Rights to Action', http://wales.gov.uk/topics/childrenyoung people/rights/sevencoreaims/?lang=en (accessed October 2010).

World Health Organisation (2001) *Mental Health: New Understanding; New Hope*. Geneva: World Health Organisation, www.who.int/whr/2001/en/ (accessed September 2011).

Chapter 9

Creativity

Dominic Wyse

Chapter summary

Creativity is increasingly recognised as an important part of educational curricula and of high value to society. There are many who regard creativity to be a unique emphasis within curricula in the UK. This, in part, may be attributed to some of the trends outlined in Chapter 2 on the history of primary education.

Research on creativity within the curriculum has focused, in particular, on how creativity should be defined and how greater creativity might be encouraged across the whole curriculum. This chapter reviews some of that research. It highlights the importance of accurate definitions and offers a succinct operational definition that informs the chapter. The central part of the chapter compares the ways that creativity is represented in the national curriculum of the countries of the UK, and briefly in a wider study of 27 countries in the European Union. The chapter also includes an analysis of the impact of England's Creative Partnerships initiative. The practical use of key ideas such as newness, value and consensual judgement of creativity are explored in order to suggest productive and practical ways to build on theory, informed by coherent definitions and understandings of creativity.

Many questions have been asked about creativity, but two of the most frequent ones are, how do we define creativity, and, can it be taught? More progress has been made on the first question than the second. The advances in knowledge about creativity have included a recognition that complete unanimity in defining it is neither possible nor necessary, due to an increased acceptance that a fundamental aspect of creativity is about *judgement*. Identifying creativity requires a judgement to be made by those who are appropriately qualified to do so. Qualification to judge creativity varies according to the nature of creativity to be judged. People qualified to judge everyday creativity are different from those qualified to judge exceptional creativity. For example, a teacher may be well qualified to judge pupils' creativity, whereas people with a high level of knowledge about art are more appropriately qualified to judge the historical contribution of someone like Tracey Emin to the discipline of art. Judgements about exceptional creativity generally require some form of consensus, in relation to a field and its historical development. Consensus is similarly a valuable, but not essential, tool for judging everyday creativity.

The recognition that creativity is partly based on judgement is not a form of naive relativism, implying that more succinct definitions have no value. On the contrary, succinct definitions of creativity are required in order to 'measure' and/or evaluate creativity. One definition that has proved to be influential is that of Vernon (1989, p. 94), who proposed that: 'Creativity means a person's capacity to produce new or original ideas, insights, restructurings, inventions, or artistic objects, which are accepted by experts as being of scientific, aesthetic, social, or technological value.' The idea that creativity requires originality is important. However originality does not exist in a vacuum, it is inspired by the field of thought that has gone before it, and that surrounds it in its present. A key question for people, as they judge something, is the extent to which it is original or not: this of course can be subject to much disagreement. Like other psychologically oriented perspectives, Vernon's view reflects a belief that creativity resides with the 'person'. However the idea that creativity has to be 'accepted' by others points to later ideas about the significance of the social context for creativity.

The Oxford English Dictionary (OED) definition of creativity, 'Creative power or faculty; ability to create' begs the question, how do we define *creative*? Used as an adjective the OED definition describes being creative as, 'Having the quality of creating, given to creating; of or pertaining to creation; originative' which naturally is closely linked to the definition for 'creativity'. When creative is used as a noun, it can refer to, for example, a person whose job involves creative work or creative material, for example, produced for advertising campaigns. The use of creative, in the context of 'the creative was designed by agency Saatchi and Saatchi', for example, refers to the materials used. The 'ability to create', which is part of the definition of creativity, is a seemingly straightforward and attractive idea for our purposes. Anybody can create something therefore everybody can be creative: creativity is a human ability.

How then does the OED define the verb 'create'? '1. a. *trans.* Said of the divine agent: To bring into being, cause to exist; *esp.* to produce where nothing was before, "to form out of nothing"'. The creation of the universe and everything is of course the most extreme form of sublime creativity (and incidentally, Haydn's depiction of the birth of the universe in his work *The Creation* is itself one of the most remarkable moments in western classical music)! The more everyday meaning is: '2. a. *gen.* To make, form, constitute, or bring into legal existence (an institution, condition, action, mental product, or form, not existing before). Sometimes of material works'. In this definition we see clear links with academic writing on the subject. Something has to be created: this thing is a product, in its widest sense, meaning a new way of thinking and/or a physical entity. Dictionary definitions serve to uphold conventions of language use in relatively succinct linguistic units through etymological and semantic analysis based on corpora of language use. The importance of succinctness should not be underestimated, in view of the need for operational definitions of creativity. Operational definitions are particularly useful in the context of assessing programmes designed to enhance creativity. In order to assess the extent to which creativity has been enhanced it is necessary to define creativity. The definitions that I use for this chapter are:

Creativity: a person's ability to create something that is regarded by appropriately qualified people as new and of value.

Creative (adjective): showing the ability to create something that is regarded by appropriately qualified people as new and of value.

Key questions for reflection

How do you interpret the meaning of the definition of creativity given in this chapter?

Think of an example of classroom practice that you regard as creative: how would you evaluate the example in relation to the definition of creativity?

Defining creativity

According to psychologists the modern era for creativity research began with J.P. Guilford's address to the American Psychological Association in 1949. Guilford began by making a close link between abilities and creative people, something he also described as a series of character traits. He described the neglect of the study of creativity as 'appalling' (Guilford, 1987, p. 34). Guilford noted the importance of creative talent to industry, science, engineering and government. A key feature of his presentation was that creativity can be expected 'however feeble, of almost all individuals' (p. 36). He argued that, up to that point, researchers had emphasised convergent thinking skills and had ignored divergent thinking skills. The use of the word 'creativity' in the title of the presentation and subsequent paper was used to sum up the kind of divergent thinking that he had in mind. In 1957 the Soviets launched the first artificial space satellite and the Americans saw a lack of creativity as one of the reasons for their failure to win the first event in the space race (Cropley, 2001). This had the effect of galvanising the field of creativity research.

Psychological research through the 1970s and 1980s was largely concerned with more detailed attempts to define and ultimately measure creativity. The 'Torrance tests of creativity' were one of the most well-known examples of such measurement. Feldman and Benjamin (2006) locate this work in the tradition of psychometric assessment and point out that the frequently cited ideas of 'technological inventiveness' and 'ideational fluency' emerged from this strand of research. However, like so many standardised tests the Torrance tests of creativity came under increasing criticism due to the telling argument that creativity was much more complex than even these well thought through tests were showing. As a result, more recent research has shown some lines of enquiry that are of particular use to educational practitioners.

Csikszentmihályi's early work, for example, focused on personality, motivation and the discovery of new problems (Csikszentmihályi, 1990). His research with several hundred artists sought to understand why some produced work that would be judged to be creative, while others did not. As far as personality was concerned it was found that more creative students tended to be more self-sufficient and not particularly interested in social norms or acceptance and tended to exhibit greater sensitivity and openness to experiences and impulses. However, the trait that most consistently distinguished these artists from others was 'a cold and aloof disposition' (1990, p. 192).

Like other researchers Csikszentmihályi and his team failed to find any relationship between traditional measures of intelligence and criteria for creative accomplishment. Csikszentmihályi realised that for many creative individuals the *formulation* of a problem is more important than its solution. Thus he set out to investigate the *discovery orientation* of artists. When presented with visually interesting objects and drawing materials a group of students were encouraged to do what they wanted, and finish when they had produced a drawing that they liked. The variables used to measure the students' discovery orientation included the number of objects that they touched: the higher the number the more likely the problem was being approached from a discovery orientation. Another variable was the number of changes the person introduced into the drawing process. Established artists and teachers rated drawings produced by students who had used discovery orientation more highly in terms of originality than other students who had used a more predictable problem-solving approach. In terms of artistic career success some seven years later the correlation was still significant.

Csikszentmihályi's early work, through a person-centred approach, led ultimately to the view that this was not the full picture. Instead he proposed that the usual question 'what is creativity?' may have to be replaced by 'where is creativity?' (Csikszentmihályi, 1990, p. 200). His well-known 'systems perspective' (p. 205) viewed creativity as the result of interaction between three subsystems: the person, the field and the domain. The domain is a system that has a set of rules. This might be a subject like mathematics, or a religion, a game, or a sport. For example western classical music is a 'domain' that requires the composition of sound and silence to create pieces of music for the benefit of performers and audiences. The 'field' is part of the social system which has the power to influence the structure of the domain. Music competitions such as the *Lionel Tertis international viola competition and workshop* are part of the way that the field of classical music has influence. Entry to music colleges and the scholarships that they provide are also part of the influence of the field. The most important function of the field is to maintain the domain as it is, but the field will also act as a gatekeeper to allow changes to the domain to take place. The role of the person is to provide variations in the domain which will be judged by the field. Variations of this kind represent exceptional creativity.

Teaching creativity

There are hundreds of programmes that claim to enhance children's creative development. These range from detailed approaches carried out over quite lengthy periods of time to specific techniques, such as SCAMPER, which encourages novelty by Substituting, Combining, Adapting, Magnifying, Putting to a different use, Eliminating, and Rearranging/Reversing (Cropley, 2001). Another example is the use of brainstorming which has been extended to include more structured ways of generating ideas, such as mind-maps and other visual techniques which use hierarchies of categories. Many of the packages begin their lives in the business sector, such as Edward de Bono's lateral thinking approach. However, in spite of great interest in the area and much financial success for some approaches the psychological literature lacks 'A clear, unequivocal, and incontestable answer to the question of how creativity can be enhanced' (Nicholson, 1999, p. 407).

Teresa Amabile has made significant contribution to the creativity research field. Because of her dissatisfaction with standardised creativity tests she used tests/activities that required the creation of some kind of real world product, for example, making paper collages or writing haiku. These were then judged by experts, such as studio artists or practising poets who rated the collages for creativity and other dimensions. Amabile called this process 'consensual assessment' (Amabile, 1990, p. 65). The conceptual definition of creativity that she used was: 'A product or response will be judged as creative to the extent that (a) it is both novel and appropriate, useful, correct, or valuable response to the task at hand, and (b) the task is heuristic rather than algorithmic' (p. 66). Amabile made the point that, although creativity is often very difficult for judges to define, they can recognise creativity when they see it. They also have considerable agreement about their judgements, particularly with products, but less so with creativity in persons or creative processes. She also argued, correctly in our view, that creativity is a continuous rather than discontinuous quality which begins at one end of the creative scale with everyday creativity and ends with Einstein, Mozart and Picasso at the other end. The difference is not the presence of creativity per se but the ability, cognitive style, motivational levels and circumstances of the different people concerned.

Beth Hennessey worked with Amabile and subsequently developed the research to make links with motivation. Hennessey has shown that intrinsic motivation enhances children's creativity, whereas extrinsic motivation, stimulated by an external goal, can be a 'killer' of creativity. For example, high stakes accountability systems have a negative effect on teachers' capacity to engage pupils' intrinsic motivation. However, Hennessey's research also showed that, to a certain extent, this negative effect can be mitigated by 'immunisation procedures' (Hennessey, 2010, p. 343). These procedures involve teachers helping children to understand the value of intrinsic motivation, in spite of a range of extrinsic motivators that may be present in classrooms. Hennessey says that this approach only maintained baseline motivation and creativity, not the unusually high levels of intrinsic motivation and creativity that are possible in the ideal classroom environment. Hennessey advocates the open classroom of the 1970s in the United States, inspired by the British infant classroom model of the 1960s, as the ideal practical realisation of what she and her colleagues have discovered about the optimal classroom conditions for creativity.

Overall, researchers remain optimistic that creativity can be enhanced by the ways that teachers work with pupils and students. A number of factors have been identified which focus on the need to:

- Reward curiosity and exploration;
- Build motivation, particularly internal motivation;
- Encourage risk-taking;
- Have high expectations/beliefs about the creative potential of students: this applies to both teachers' views of their pupils, and pupils' own self image;

- Give opportunities for choice and discovery – 'The evidence is fairly compelling, and not surprising, that people are more interested in – more internally motivated to engage in – activities they have chosen for themselves, than activities that have been selected for them by others, or in which they are obliged to engage for reasons beyond their control' (Dudek and Côté, 1994; Kohn, 1993)'
- Develop students' self-management skills
- Support domain specific knowledge: pupils need to understand as much as possible about the domain (for example, the subject area) that they are doing the creative work in.

(Nicholson, 1999, p. 409)

This point about opportunities for choice is highly significant and one which the English education system has repeatedly neglected, particularly since 1988, but as we show in this book it has formal recognition in Scotland's curriculum.

Key questions for reflection

How would you put into practice the factors expressed in the Nicholson (1999) bullet points?

Creative partnerships

In 1999 the government-commissioned report *All Our Futures: Creativity, Culture and Education* (the NACCCE Report) (NACCCE, 1999) argued that a national strategy for creative and cultural education was essential to unlock the potential of every young person. One of the most positive developments following the NACCCE report was the national *Creative Partnerships* (CP) initiative which

> brings creative workers such as artists, architects and scientists into schools to work with teachers to inspire young people and help them learn. The programme has worked with over 1 million children, and over 90,000 teachers in more than 8000 projects in England since 2002. Creative Partnerships is England's flagship creative learning programme, designed to develop the skills of children and young people across England, raising their aspirations, achievements and life chances.
>
> (Creativity, Culture and Education, 2011, online)

CP's initial commitment to grassroots control of creative projects was unique in the sense that most other educational initiatives generated by the New Labour government of 1997 to 2010 generally featured heavy top-down control. Although the government failed to implement some of the most important recommendations of the NACCCE report, it invested significantly in Creative Partnerships.

Two large-scale national evaluations of CP were commissioned. The evaluation addressing the link between attainment and creative partnerships projects found a modest impact at key stage three and key stage four but not at key stage two (Kendall *et al.*, 2008). It should be noted that the measure of attainment used was the national statutory test scores, which are not the most appropriate measure for the impact of initiatives that sought to encourage *creative learning*. The second evaluation looked at the impact of creative partnerships on teachers, which was overwhelmingly positive. Interestingly, teachers felt that CP had particularly benefited the development of skills for leadership and interpersonal work. Those who had experienced higher levels of involvement in CP not surprisingly felt that there had been more impact than those who had less involvement.

Some of the earliest evaluations of CP were carried out regionally in Merseyside and Manchester/Salford between 2003 and 2005 (Wyse and Spendlove, 2007). The work advanced understanding of what was a new term in the context of a policy initiative, *creative learning*. It was not clear why creative learning had been selected in preference to creativity as the main idea behind CP. It became apparent from the research that there was uncertainty about the meaning of creative learning for those involved with CP. Hence, one of the outcomes of the analyses of participants' perceptions and of creativity theory and research, was to offer a working definition of creative learning as: 'learning which leads to new or original thinking which is accepted by appropriate observers as being of value'.

Specifying, even in a preliminary way, the meaning of the terms *creative* and *learning* and how they relate to each other was welcomed (Craft *et al.*, 2008). The work in Merseyside also generated insights into barriers to creativity. There was an overriding feeling from teachers involved that creative learning represented something less formal and less restrictive than much of the practice that was prevalent at the time. The two most significant barriers to creative practice were perceived to be the assessment system and the national curriculum, particularly the national strategies. Jones and Wyse (2004) highlighted the tension between standards and creativity that were part of England's Department for Education and Skills national strategy *Excellence and Enjoyment* (DfES, 2003). These findings were echoed to a certain extent by the idea of an interaction between *performativity* and creativity policies (Troman *et al.*, 2007 – Jeffrey and Woods had been researching creative teaching and creative learning from an educational perspective at least since 1996). The idea that curriculum and assessment policy could create barriers to creativity was not accepted by government. In response to the Roberts report, commissioned to review creativity in schools, the government reiterated its position that 'creativity and standards go hand in hand' (Department for Culture, Media and Sport, 2006, p. 4).

In spite of the overall success of CP over its lifetime, including admiration for Creative Partnerships shown in a House of Commons Education Select Committee report backed up by the New Labour government's response, ultimately government funding for CP was cut by the Conservative–Liberal Democrat coalition government from 2011.

Creativity and national curricula

In 2010 the European Commission published the final report on its study of creativity and innovation (Institute for Prospective Technological Studies (IPTS), Cachia *et al.*,

2010). The study addressed the role of creativity in primary and secondary education in 27 member states of the European Union. The findings in relation to curricula included the perception that there was in general insufficient encouragement for creativity, caused in many cases by a lack of clear definitions and understanding. The findings also showed that excessive curriculum content was regarded as a common barrier to creativity. In spite of commitment to curricula, frequently stated by teachers, conventional teaching methods such as 'chalk and talk' were an obstacle to creativity because this kind of formal teaching is less likely to lead to creativity. Primary teachers were considered to be more likely than secondary teachers to promote creative learning and active learner-centred approaches in class. Summative assessment processes were recognised as a barrier while more versatile assessment processes were perceived as an enabler. Revision of curricula to include more creativity therefore requires parallel revisions in assessment systems if creativity is to flourish. Within the UK the IPTS study noted that Northern Ireland and Scotland's curriculum texts had the most prominent use of the term creativity.

You will remember from Chapter 3 that creativity featured in the aims for the primary national curriculum in England from 1999 onwards. The handbook and accompanying website also included creativity in 'Promoting skills across the curriculum' as part of a thinking skills section. At a later date an extra section called 'Learning across the curriculum' was added to the online version of the national curriculum. This section contained extensive requirements and guidance about how creativity could be fostered in the curriculum. In 2010, following the Rose review of the primary curriculum, commissioned by the New Labour government, a new primary curriculum was published online which required pupils 'to create', 'to develop creativity skills' and 'to develop creativity'. However, in 2011 the new coalition government set aside these recommendations and initiated yet another review of the national curriculum. The website outlining the Rose recommendations was removed and archived because it was no longer recognised as government policy. At the same time the guidance on 'promoting skills across the curriculum material' was also removed from the national curriculum website because it was deemed non-statutory.

In Wales, the foundation phase curriculum includes creativity as part of thinking skills in its 'Skills across the curriculum' section. 'Developing thinking' is described as thinking across the curriculum through the processes of planning, developing and reflecting in order that pupils can make sense of their world. It is argued that these processes enable children to think creatively and critically. Uniquely, Wales includes 'Creative Development' as a discrete foundation stage 'area of learning'. This is summarised as follows:

> Children should be continually developing their imagination and creativity across the curriculum. Their natural curiosity and disposition to learn should be stimulated by everyday sensory experiences, both indoors and outdoors. Children should engage in creative, imaginative and expressive activities in art, craft, design, music, dance and movement. Children should explore a wide range of stimuli, develop their ability to communicate and express their creative ideas, and reflect on their work.
>
> (Department for Children, Education,
> Lifelong Learning and Skills, 2008, p. 10)

In addition Wales' 'Skills framework for 3 to 19-year-olds' includes the claim that the developing thinking section of the framework is underpinned by creative and critical thinking although metacognition seems to be the strongest focus.

Northern Ireland also locates creativity within its 'Thinking Skills and Personal Capabilities' framework which advocates the provision of worthwhile experiences across the curriculum that allow pupils to develop skills, including being creative. Examples include seeking questions and problems to solve, making new connections, valuing the unexpected, and taking risks.

Unlike the other nations Scotland does not have a separate and explicit framework promoting thinking skills and creativity, instead creativity is built into the experiences and outcomes across the curriculum areas. Scotland also includes a 'Learning across the curriculum' section but creativity is not identified as a separate strand as it is in Wales and was in England.

The strongest commitment to creativity as evident from national curricula is seen in Wales' national curriculum, particularly in its identification of a separate area of learning to complement the inclusion of creativity as part of thinking skills. However, Scotland's inclusion of creativity as a theme that is built into the experiences and outcomes is perhaps the most logical conception because creativity is a process and disposition rather than a subject/area of learning. Although the inclusion of creativity as part of thinking skills in three of the nations is welcome there is a danger that this categorisation of creativity is somewhat limited. Although creativity is characterised by divergent thinking this is only one important part of what it means to be creative. However, its inclusion in thinking skills sections in national curricula is often characterised by additional descriptions that indicate a much broader understanding of creativity.

Implications for practice

As we have shown in this chapter, creativity is a part of all national curriculula in the four nations but there are also barriers to teachers and pupils engaging most fully with creativity as a result of extrinsic factors such as high stakes testing systems and over-reliance on top-down curriculum control. But it is not only researchers who have been critical of policy, wider society has also expressed grave concerns. For example, five leading children's authors voiced their concerns personally to the government in England and left readers in little doubt about their dismay. Phillip Pullman described the curriculum for young people as 'brutal', and suggested that we are creating a generation of children who hate reading and who 'feel nothing but hostility for literature' (Ward, 2003). In his view:

> There are no rules. Anything that's any good has to be discovered in the process of writing it . . . we cannot require everything to take place under the glare of discussion and checking and testing and consultation: some things have to be private and tentative. Teaching at its best can give pupils the confidence to discover this mysterious state and to begin to explore the things that can be discovered there.
>
> (Pullman, 2003, p. 2)

Anne Fine felt that there had been 'a real drop in the standard of children's writing – not in grammar, construction or spelling, but in the untestable quality of creativity' (Katbamna, 2003, p. 3) Booker prize winner Ben Okri used the opportunity provided by *The Times Educational Supplement* in its 'My Best Teacher' section to voice his frustration with the education system:

> I think the culture of education is wrong. It is too much like a production line – you're doing this so at the end of the day you'll be doing that . . . For the past 10 years I have been trying to find someone to teach me how to swim, and it has led me to thinking that the great problem of teaching is that people have forgotten how to learn. We're not learners any more, we're collectors of facts. People tell me, 'Do it this way, do it that way', and whenever I do, I end up nearly drowning.
>
> (Okri, 2000, p. 7)

Many of the problems identified by these writers chime with findings from curriculum research and scholarship into teaching today. If we accept that some of these issues are real then what can and should teachers do to improve creativity in the classroom?

Key questions for reflection

What should teachers do to improve creativity in the classroom?

First and foremost, creativity is best understood as being about the key components of newness and value. Teachers should engage pupils with classroom activities and learning that encourage them to create ideas and products that exhibit newness and that are valued. The teacher and the class are highly appropriate 'judges' of these components. It is not absolute unanimity about creativity that is important, but the process of creating, then thinking and discussing what is new and what is of value.

Special creativity programmes are not needed but more the commitment of teachers to some basic ideas. One of these is that everyone exhibits creativity to different degrees and in different areas. However, teachers' advocacy of and encouragement of intrinsic motivation, and challenges to the worst features of extrinsic motivation, such as high stakes testing and performance cultures, is vital. We should look to the logic of Scotland's inclusion of creativity as a theme informing the whole curriculum, and to the commitment to creativity evident in the national curricula of Northern Ireland and Wales, and hope that England's review of its national curriculum will not result in minimising the place of creativity in a country that historically has an internationally renowned reputation for its curricula that celebrate creativity.

Teacher education/training task

Choose one area of the national curriculum that requires teachers to encourage pupils' creativity. Plan a scheme of work that would address the requirement.

Further reading

Creativity, Culture and Education (2011) *About Creative Partnerships*. Available from www.creative-partnerships.com/about.
Explore the CCE website for examples of creative work in schools.

Hennessey, B. (2010) Intrinsic Motivation and Creativity in the Classroom: Have We Come Full Circle? In R. Beghetto and J. Kaufman (eds), *Nurturing Creativity in the Classroom*. Cambridge: Cambridge University Press, pp. 342–365.
A rich account of Hennessey's long career of research on a key aspect of creativity.

Jones, R. and Wyse, D. (eds) (forthcoming) *Creativity in the Primary Curriculum* (Second Edition). London: David Fulton.
Shows how creativity can be enhanced in the different subjects of the curriculum.

References

Amabile, T. (1990) Within You, Without You: The Social Psychology of Creativity, and Beyond. In M. Runco and R. Albert (eds), *Theories of Creativity*. London: Sage, pp. 215–233.

Cachia, R., Ferrari, A., Ala-Mutka, K. and Punie, Y. (2010) Creative Learning and Innovative Teaching. Final Report on the Study on Creativity and Innovation in Education in the EU Member States. Seville: European Commission. Joint Research Centre. Institute for Prospective Technological Studies (IPTS).

Craft, A., Cremin, T. and Burnard, P. (eds) (2008) *Creative Learning 3–11: And How We Document it*. Stoke-on-Trent: Trentham.

Cropley, A.J. (2001) *Creativity in Education and Learning: A Guide for Teachers and Educators*. London: Kogan Page.

Csikszentmihályi, M. (1990) The Domain of Creativity. In M. Runco and R. Albert (eds), *Theories of Creativity*. London: Sage, pp. 190–214.

Creativity, Culture and Education (2011) *About Creative Partnerships*. Available from www.creative-partnerships.com/about/.

Department for Children, Education, Lifelong Learning and Skills (2008) *Framework for Children's Learning for 3 to 7-year olds in Wales*. Cardiff: Welsh Assembly Government.

Department for Culture, Media and Sport (DfCMS) and Department for Education and Skills (DfEE) (2006) *Government Response to Paul Roberts' Report on Nurturing Creativity in Young People*. London: Department for Culture, Media and Sport (DfCMS)/Department for Education and Skills (DfEE).

Department for Education and Skills (DfES) (2003) *Excellence and Enjoyment: A Strategy for Primary Schools*. Nottingham: DfES Publications.

Feldman, D.H. and Benjamin, A. (2006) Creativity and Education: An American Retrospective. *Cambridge Journal of Education*, 36(3): 319–336.

Guilford, J.P. (1987) Creativity Research: Past, Present and Future. In S.G. Isaksen (ed.), *Frontiers of Creativity Research*. New York: Bearly Limited, pp. 341–379.

Hennessey, B. (2010). Intrinsic Motivation and Creativity in the Classroom: Have We Come Full Circle? In R. Beghetto and J. Kaufman (eds), *Nurturing Creativity in the Classroom*. Cambridge: Cambridge University Press, pp. 342–365.

Jones, R. and Wyse, D. (eds) (2004) *Creativity in the Primary Curriculum.* London: David Fulton.

Katbamna, M. (2003) Crisis of Creativity. *Guardian Education,* 30 September.

Kendall, L., Morrison, J., Yeshanew, T. and Sharp, C. (2008) *The Longer-Term Impact of Creative Partnerships on the Attainment of Young People: Results from 2005 and 2006.* Slough: NFER.

National Advisory Committee on Creative and Cultural Education (NACCCE) (1999) *All Our Futures: Creativity, Culture and Education.* Suffolk: DfEE Publications.

Nicholson, R.S. (1999) Enhancing Creativity. In R.J. Sternberg (ed.), *Handbook of Creativity.* Cambridge: Cambridge University Press, pp. 392–430.

Okri, B. (2000) My Best Teacher (in discussion with Hilary Wilce). *Times Educational Supplement* (Friday Section), 19 September, p. 7.

Pullman, P. (2003) Lost the Plot. *Guardian Education,* 30 September.

Troman, G., Jeffrey, B. and Raggl, A. (2007) Creativity and Performativity Policies in Primary School Cultures. *Journal of Education Policy,* 22(5): 549–572.

Vernon, P. (1989) The Nature-Nurture Problem in Creativity. In J. Glover, R. Ronning and C. Reynolds (eds), *Handbook of Creativity.* London: Plenum Press, pp. 93–110.

Ward, L. (2003) Tests are Making Children Hate Books. *Guardian Education,* 30 November.

Wyse, D. and Spendlove, D. (2007) Partners in Creativity: Action Research and Creative Partnerships. *Education 3–13,* 35(2): 181–191.

Chapter 10

Curriculum for the future

Moira Hulme and Kay Livingston

Chapter summary

This chapter offers a synoptic overview of the key themes presented in this collection and offers some recommendations for the primary curriculum of the future. Drawing on processes of curriculum making in the four countries of the UK, the chapter revisits the issues of curriculum control, professional autonomy and responsibility. Consideration is given to the role of enquiry within teachers' professional development and the need to reassert the critical relationship between curriculum development and teacher development.

Introduction

There are two main sections to this final chapter. The first section addresses renewed interest in teachers as curriculum inquirers and schools as curriculum agencies. Here discussion focuses on the balance between central direction (government policy for schools and national curricula frameworks) and professional discretion to meet local needs (school-level decision making, curriculum flexibility). Enhanced responsibilities and opportunities for curriculum innovation and review by teachers are considered. The second section addresses the value and limits of cross-national comparison in curriculum development. Areas of convergence and divergence are identified and the political basis of curriculum making is stressed, particularly the extent to which curriculum policy can be said to be evidence-based and informed by consultation. Throughout this collection we have argued that the primary curriculum for the future needs to address approaches to teaching and learning ('pedagogy'), the ways in which children and their learning are assessed, and the contexts in which they live and learn. This is best achieved through an aims-informed and process-driven approach to the curriculum. Developing the curriculum from this perspective requires a strong commitment to teacher development, professional inquiry and values-clarification.

Teachers as curriculum makers and schools as curriculum agencies

In Chapter 4 we saw how an 'inquiry stance' (Cochran-Smith and Lytle, 2009) supports the continuing professional growth of teachers. If teacher education is conceived as acquiring a narrow set of competencies (on qualifying to teach), rather than a commitment to career-long learning, the capacity of teachers to act as curriculum makers is reduced. The period from the mid-1980s to devolution saw the diminution of local variation in the curriculum in each of the four jurisdictions of the UK. Throughout this period traditions of school-based curriculum development and collaborative partnerships between schools and other bodies in processes of curriculum review were diminished in moves to establish strong curricular frameworks across the UK that assured 'entitlement'.

Over time the pendulum has perhaps swung back towards greater curricula flexibility, local discretion and decision making. In Scotland *Curriculum for Excellence* offers more scope for professional autonomy than its predecessor, *Curriculum 5–14*. In Wales and Northern Ireland curriculum prescription was relaxed following devolution, especially in the earlier years of schooling. Much has been made of the 'new freedoms' to be enjoyed by schools and teachers in recent reforms, as exemplified in the pronouncements of *The Importance of Teaching* in England (Department for Education, 2010) and *Teaching Scotland's Future* (Donaldson, 2011). These documents offer radically divergent views on a socially just education system but both accentuate the professional responsibilities of teachers as local decision makers. *Teaching Scotland's Future* repeatedly positions teachers as 'co-creators of the curriculum' (p.4) and 'agents of change, not passive or reluctant receivers of externally-imposed prescription' (p.19).

> Curriculum for Excellence is much more than a reform of curriculum and assessment. It is predicated on a model of sustained change which sees schools and teachers as co-creators of the curriculum.
>
> (Donaldson, 2011, p.4)

> It should be for teachers, not government, to design the lessons and the experiences which will engage students. Government can help by clearing away the clutter of unnecessary curricular detail, and restricting itself to outlining the core knowledge children should expect to acquire.
>
> (Department for Education, 2010, p.46)

There are a number of contradictory strains within *The Importance of Teaching*. It follows the decision of the Conservative–Liberal Democrat coalition government in January 2011 to initiate a review of the National Curriculum, the fourth major review of the primary curriculum in England in three years. On the one hand, it is argued 'the [English] National Curriculum includes too much that is not essential knowledge, and there is too much prescription about how to teach' (2010, p.10). On the other, the government is to specify more tightly 'the core knowledge children should expect to acquire' (p.46) and promote adoption of 'the best approaches to the teaching of early reading and early mathematics' (p.26) without acknowledgement of any debate about 'best approaches'. Early indications in England suggest that scope for innovation is likely to be contained within the parameters of a traditional subject-focused curriculum, with fewer spaces for 'disruptive pedagogies' (Weis and Fine, 2001). However, new opportunities are presented in the renewed emphasis on school-level discretion. Nevertheless, capacity for curriculum inquiry may not be enhanced in compressed, skills-based school-centred programmes of initial teacher education.

The United Kingdom is not alone in responding to these challenges. Law and Nieveen (2010, p.6) suggest that international trends on curriculum reform require educators to 'balance central direction with adaptation to meet particular local needs'. Tatto (2007) has described how a repertoire of global reforms has sought to increase control over teachers' work and performance whilst simultaneously emphasising teachers' knowledge and discretion. Within this mix, relations of partnership will become increasingly important in determining whether professional or managerial forms of accountability will dominate in the future. Professional accountability entails self-regulation, such as through professional codes of conduct. Managerial accountability is associated with external controls of audit and performance management, for example through examination performance ('league') tables.

Increased flexibility to adapt the curriculum and classroom instruction to meet individual needs places greater demands on teachers' pedagogical competence. In Scotland, two recent reports on teacher education and teachers' work – Donaldson (2011) and McCormac (2011) – highlight the need for teachers' professional commitment towards their own professional development to raise the quality of education. Donaldson (2011) recommended that a more relevant, sustained and effective approach to professional development was needed within a culture of 'pull' from teachers rather than 'push' from outside the classroom (Donaldson, 2011, p.10). McCormac (2011, p.6) picks up this theme, suggesting that professionalism 'depends crucially on all teachers embracing professional obligations which go beyond that which can or should be embodied in a contract'. McCormac (2011) has emphasised the need for a combination of policy and professional responses to educational challenges. 'Ensuring our education system anticipates and addresses the rapidly changing and highly variable educational needs of children is a central professional and policy concern' (McCormac, 2011, p.5).

Expectations of 'extended professionalism' (Hoyle, 1974) present new challenges in identifying how best to support teachers' continuing professional learning in times of significant change when individual learning needs are diverse. As teachers are positioned as curriculum makers they assume new responsibilities. Not all schools and teachers are equally well placed to take on these new roles. Addressing the problem of content overload in the school curriculum gives rise to new challenges of professional support. In the absence of adequately resourced forms of tailored support, content-overload might quickly be replaced by teacher-overload. What is needed is more support for school-based professional development, particularly as research suggests that CPD is most effective when it is site-based, fits with school culture and ethos, addresses particular needs of teachers, is peer-led, collaborative and sustained (Menter *et al.*, 2010). Building capacity for curriculum innovation by teachers requires sustained opportunities for collaboration between teachers and researchers and partnership work between the various bodies involved in curriculum development and teacher development.

Teacher-to-teacher, inter-school, cross-sectoral and inter-agency collaboration are features of effective partnership work. Advances have been made in the development of: (1) local authority and teacher learning communities; (2) school-based coaching and mentoring initiatives, supported by external consultants and critical friends; and (3) through the promotion of inclusive 'communities for learning' in innovative teacher education partnerships (Livingston and Colucci-Gray, 2006). In addition, grassroots teacher-led initiatives have grown in the UK such as the face-to-face and electronic (un)conferences, Teach Meets. This demonstrates teachers' commitment to developing their professional learning and to building peer relationships in the learning process.

Teacher learning communities (TLCs) have played an important role in promoting learning *how* to learn through Assessment *for* Learning (AfL). Dylan Wiliam (2007) advocates teacher learning communities to address the issue of 'routinisation' in teaching (year on year repetition of the same routines or habits with a loss of creativity, questioning and experimentation). Wiliam (2007, p.196) has argued that, '[t]eachers learn most of what they know about teaching before they are 18 years old'. Coming together to question practice helps teachers to continue to problematise their classroom practice and to develop expertise through experience. Teacher learning communities enable their members to work collaboratively to share experiences, new knowledge and skills in a supportive environment. Strong trusting relationships enable peer observation and dialogue about learning and teaching approaches and support in taking next steps. This follows Assessment for Learning processes where evidence collected through peer observation can support changes to curriculum or changes to the proposed pedagogy. Chapter 5 on assessment pointed out that Assessment for Learning is also assessment for teachers' learning. Assessment for Learning is the process of seeking and interpreting evidence for use by learners and their teachers to decide where the learners are in their learning, where they need to go and how best to get there (Assessment Reform Group, 2002, pp.2–3).

Peer mentoring provides opportunities for analysis and dialogue about learning and teaching within the context of a teacher's own classroom. It moves professional development from generic and sometimes abstract topics to those tailor-made to the specific needs of a teacher and her pupils. A national framework for coaching and mentoring in England was developed in 2004–5 and distinguishes between:

- Mentoring: a structured, sustained process for supporting professional learners through significant career transitions;
- Specialist Coaching: a structured, sustained process for enabling the development of a specific aspect of a professional learner's practice; and
- Collaborative (Co-)Coaching: a structured, sustained process between two or more professional learners to enable them to embed new knowledge and skills from specialist sources in day-to-day practice.

(CUREE, 2005, p.3)

The Centre for the Use of Research and Evidence in Education (CUREE, www.curee. co.uk) has developed a suite of professional development resources to support Effective

Mentoring and Coaching. The National College employs coaching within its leadership development programmes. Peer coaching typically involves observing lessons and creating opportunities for professional dialogue. Case studies of schools that have worked to develop a coaching culture are available from the National College website (www.national college.org.uk). For interesting case studies of inter-professional collaboration and community involvement in local curriculum making see the concept of an 'area-based curriculum' proposed in the RSA (Royal Society for the Encouragement of Arts, Manufactures and Commerce) pilot projects, the Manchester curriculum and the Peterborough curriculum (www.thersa.org/projects/education/area-based-curriculum). There has been a similar emphasis on the development of peer mentoring in Scotland with pilot projects underway in several local authorities. Through peer mentoring teachers are discussing curriculum content, pedagogy and assessment approaches, learning from one another and improving learning and teaching within the context of *Curriculum for Excellence*.

Key questions for reflection

What opportunities are available for collaborative professional learning in your locality?

To what extent does evidence play a part in your decision about the curriculum and its teaching?

Think of an example of collaboration that you have been involved with. What made the collaboration more or less successful?

In the schools that you have worked in to what extent would you say that the curriculum is locally developed?

University Schools of Education occupy a pivotal role in bridging divisions between members of the education community; promoting the integration of curriculum theory, with curriculum innovation and evaluation, and teachers' decision making in the classroom. In Scotland, the Donaldson Review (2011) places strong emphasis on the need for effective education to be developed through a partnership model with schools, local authorities, universities and others working together. This is a challenging approach particularly if different views and values are held about purpose, content and learning and teaching approaches.

Positive illustrations of collaborative curriculum development are found among a range of diverse international examples. Curriculum reform in Finland from 1994 has increased teachers' participation in curricular decision making and enabled the construction of school-specific policies. A research-orientation to teacher education and curriculum development is encouraged through established links between training schools and university Schools of Education. Curriculum reform in Norway from 2007 has given teachers greater freedom of choice over teaching methods and has promoted collaborative work to build schools' capacity for organisational change. Practice-based research and development projects have sought to involve practitioners in setting research priorities and in conducting collaborative enquiries (Salo *et al.*, 2008). In New Zealand, devolution of responsibility for curriculum decisions to schools has been accompanied by the development of self-review tools for teachers, such as the teacher Inquiry and knowledge building cycle articulated by Timperley *et al.* (2007). In Australia the Innovative Links project and National Schools Network promoted collaboration and reciprocal learning between researchers and teachers in mutually identified projects (Sachs, 2003).

In the Netherlands school–university collaboration is advanced through the work of The Netherlands Institute for Curriculum Development (SLO). Much can be learned from the collaborative approach to 'educational design research' advanced by SLO (van den Akker *et al.*, 2006). Design research is an iterative process, involving analysis, design and formative evaluation of prototype materials. Teachers work with researchers in classroom settings to field test curricula materials with the aim of advancing research-based improvement of professional practice. A range of participatory (and repeated) methods are employed to gather teacher and pupil perspectives on proposed changes to specific areas of the curriculum including interviews, walk-throughs, group discussions, lesson observations, reflective journals and learning logs. Design research intends to generate three outputs: design principles that can be shared ('lessons learned'), curricular products (e.g. improved teachers' guides and materials) and the professional development of participants (through opportunities for sustained professional dialogue, reflection and critical engagement). Curricular designs are evaluated through cycles of inquiry to determine how far they are 'viable' (against considerations of practicality, relevance and sustainability), 'legitimate' (research-informed) and 'effective' (in producing desired outcomes) (van den Akker, 2006).

Authentic collaboration not only contributes to the democratisation of existing partnerships, but may strengthen the warrant and credibility of proposed changes among those who are responsible for the 'enactment' of policy (Braun *et al.*, 2010), that is, teachers in the classroom. In Ontario, a core priority is increasing public confidence in publicly funded schools. Policy makers in Ontario believe that high levels of satisfaction and confidence in schools are central to establishing strong community–school partnerships and keeping the focus and energy of the education sector on improving support for student learning (Ontario, 2008). Greater collaborative development, involving enhanced teacher agency and community involvement, might support incremental and lasting change that bridges parliamentary cycles. If teachers are to respond positively to invitations to take up an extended professional role as 'co-constructors' of the curriculum, new relations of partnership and control will need to be negotiated.

Key question for reflection

How can curriculum frameworks be designed, implemented and supported to enhance pupil learning?

A curriculum for the future will make new demands on schools and teachers preparing learners for participation, employment and active citizenship in new times. The Commission of the European Communities published a working paper entitled *Schools for the 21st Century*. The paper suggested that:

> Young people can no longer expect to spend their whole lifetime in one sector of employment, or even in one place; their career paths will change in unpredictable ways, and they will need a wide range of generic competences to enable them to adapt. In an increasingly complex world, creativity, the ability to think laterally, transversal skills and adaptability tend to be values more than specific bodies of knowledge.
>
> (Commission of the European Communities, 2007, p.5)

In the paper key competences are identified which refer to the knowledge, skills and attitudes that serve for personal fulfilment, social inclusion and active citizenship and employability. It is suggested that these key competences should include the 'traditional' competences like mother tongue language, foreign languages, basic competences in maths and science, and digital competence, but also more transversal ones such as learning to learn, social and civic competence, initiative taking and entrepreneurship, and cultural awareness and expression. This curriculum framework highlights the importance of achieving breadth and depth in the curriculum and providing pupils with a strong frame of reference for their learning that enables them to self-monitor what they currently know and know how to go about the next steps in their learning. This requires teachers who understand the needs of their pupils through dialogue with them; and who are able to provide pupils with high quality teaching whilst building pupils' confidence and skills as learners. It also requires strong partnership working to enable the learner to connect to different sources of learning and opportunities to learn in different ways.

The policy makers in Ontario in the introduction to a document setting out a plan for education said:

> If we had to pick out a single word to epitomise our aspirations, it would be an education system that 'energises' everyone in it or who comes into contact with it ... This paper presents the government's plan to continue working with our partners to build and energise Ontario's schools. Together, we will reach every student and create an education system that is second to none.
>
> (Ontario, 2008, p.2)

The rhetoric of policy documents often hold great promise and it is in the implementation approaches that tensions and challenges can arise. The way that policy is interpreted and supported in schools and classrooms is central to its success. The more that teachers are involved in policy development the greater the likelihood of its success and impact on pupil learning. In Scotland, for example, teachers who were directly involved in trialling the new curriculum's experiences and outcomes in their own classrooms were more supportive of it than teachers who were not involved in the trialling process (University of Glasgow, 2009). This highlights the importance of teachers' interaction with policy frameworks and the need to make sense of them in local contexts according to the learning needs of the pupils. It also points to the importance of giving teachers greater professional freedom over how they organise and teach the curriculum. This suggests a process-driven approach to curriculum which envisages education as an interactive process of inquiry and values-clarification.

Cross-national comparison

A great deal of attention over the past two decades has focused on the international movement of ideas in education or 'policy borrowing' (Steiner-Khamsi, 2004; Phillips and Ochs, 2004; Phillips, 2006). It is commonplace to justify reform in terms of lessons learned from 'effective' practice elsewhere. Increasingly policy makers are getting together at an international level to discuss improving the quality of educational provision. For example, an international summit held in New York entitled 'Improving Teacher Quality around the World' brought together education ministers, union leaders and other teacher leaders from 16 countries to discuss and review teacher quality and to share policy developments (Asia Society, 2011). Proposed changes are often premised on what research tells us about the 'best performing' education systems. A greater volume of information about education systems across the world is now available to policy makers. Discussions at the international summit drew on country background reports prepared by the OECD and the findings of the Teaching and Learning International Survey (TALIS) (OECD, 2009). Chapters 1 and 5 indicated the way that data collected through international surveys is impacting on curriculum reforms. Information is available to policy makers though the development of international assessment systems such as PISA (Programme for International Student Assessment), PIRLS (Progress in International Reading Survey) and TIMSS (Trends in International Mathematics and Science Study). As research-aware practitioners, it is important to interrogate the claims made in policy documents and to scrutinise the warrant of findings that are used to make a case for change. Changing policy is a dynamic process and trajectories of curriculum reform are complex. Curriculum reforms may be influenced by international, national or local factors. However, the teacher working in collaboration with partners in the local context should be positioned to make decisions about the curriculum content and the learning and teaching approaches according to her pupils' abilities and needs. This requires well-informed professional teachers who are able to rework/amend/adapt the curriculum framework by taking account of their pupils, their school and their community.

The concepts of 'travelling' and 'embedded policy' are helpful in explaining how supranational themes are translated in different national contexts (Ozga and Jones, 2006; Jones and Alexiadou, 2001). Inter-UK policy making cannot be neatly disentangled from wider globalising trends. Crude 'policy borrowing' often fails to consider the particular historical, geographical, cultural, political and economic context of policy formation (Crossley and Watson, 2003). The political culture of the host country (or region) is significant in filtering and remodelling trans-national agenda. Some aspects of policy substance and language 'travel' further than others. Travelling policy is 'recontextualised' within national, regional (local authority) and institutional (school) settings (Ball, 1998).

Ozga (2005, p.2) explains that, 'Embedded policy is to be found in "local" spaces, where global policy agendas come up against existing priorities and practices'.

As we have seen in this volume, curriculum movements that appear similar can be informed by different rationales and are enacted in different ways at different times, *within* as well as *between* national and cultural borders. Policies are not transplanted intact from one jurisdiction to another but are influenced by time, place, space and pace. Whilst there are global pressures towards 'harmonisation', 'standardisation' and 'convergence', the role of the national policy community remains important in explaining how curriculum policy is shaped in local settings.

> When we look more closely at how ideas get translated into policies and practices, the differences in national contexts loom larger than the similarities. In each setting general ideas must be turned into specific regulations and practices and at this level the pressure of local circumstances comes to the fore, so that what look like similar policies end up being quite different practices.
>
> (Levin, 1998, p.135)

Chapter 1 noted that different levels of consultation on the school curriculum in different jurisdictions have produced layers of convergence and divergence. Curriculum frameworks developed in each jurisdiction of the UK from the 1980s were strongly subject-based and introduced levels of attainment. Some common 'travelling' themes in recent curriculum making include a developing focus on 'capacities' (that is, the desired learner attributes and capabilities that the curriculum seeks to develop, e.g., *successful learner, confident individual, responsible citizen* and *effective contributor*), a concern to reduce content overload, to have less rigid subject boundaries and to improve the use of assessment. Where overarching aims appear similar, national distinctiveness still applies. The aims that underpin the Scottish *Curriculum for Excellence* resemble those developed in Northern Ireland in 2001. However, a closer look at policy language reveals differences in emphasis.

Similarities in the architecture and language of national curriculum texts can obscure *differences* in interpretation and professional practice.

- As noted in Chapter 1, England and Scotland emphasise dispositions and require pupils 'to become . . .'. Northern Ireland places a strong emphasis on empowerment. The reformed curriculum in Wales places a particular emphasis on the rights of young people.
- Chapter 7 highlights the importance of language in the national curricula of each of the four jurisdictions of the UK but noted significant variation in the language requirements of the curricula of Northern Ireland, Scotland and Wales, especially in regard to talk, reading and writing.
- Chapter 8 identified that whilst personal and social education (and associated subjects) is referred to in national curricula across the UK, there is little agreement on its elements, mode of delivery or the vexing issue of assessment.
- In Chapter 9 we saw how the term 'creativity' featured more prominently within the curriculum texts for Scotland and Northern Ireland. In Wales in the Foundation

Stage the area of learning generally called the Arts in other countries has been renamed creativity, an approach which risks associating creativity with one 'area of learning'. In contrast, creativity in Scotland's *Curriculum for Excellence* is embedded within Experiences and Outcomes; it is recognised as a process and a disposition rather than discrete areas of learning.

Areas of commonality within the formal curriculum are played out in different national systems of education that are founded on different value systems (Lawton, 1989). In Chapter 2 some common themes in the history of primary schooling were identified – 'basic skills', 'subjects' (and knowledge) and 'the child'. These themes have been addressed over time in divergent settings – there is an enduring system of selective education in Northern Ireland (despite the abolition of state-sponsored selection in 2009), a larger private sector and increasingly diverse forms of school governance in England; in contrast to continued support for non-selective community comprehensive schools in Wales and Scotland.

Proposals for major curriculum reform are subject to debate by politicians, civil servants, pressure groups, think tanks and within the education community. Political sensitivities enabled differences in 'emphasis' and 'substance' to emerge following the Education Reform Act 1988 (Wallace, 1994). Responsiveness to local needs and priorities is seen in the inclusion of Education for Mutual Understanding and Cultural Heritage in Northern Ireland in 1989 and the greater prominence of 'Welshness' expressed in the Curriculum Cymreig and Welsh language provision in the curriculum in Wales. The politics of the curriculum are seen in the absence or adaptation of aspects of English orders and strategies elsewhere. The literacy and numeracy strategies, for example, were not fully developed in Wales and Northern Ireland (see Chapter 2 and Chapter 7).

Devolution of power to new assemblies in Northern Ireland and Wales and to a new parliament in Scotland in 1999 extended opportunities for divergence. Opportunities for public consultation increased through tele-democracy – online forums, citizens' panels, policy road shows – enabling 'national conversations', in addition to expert reviews and research syntheses. A comprehensive and evidence-based review of the Northern Ireland curriculum from 1996 led to the development of the Revised Curriculum between 2000 and 2003, implemented from 2007, which included four separate and robust consultations. Developments in Wales post-devolution included the abolition of national testing (2001, 2006), the introduction of the Foundation Phase (3–7 year olds) (2008), a first review of the 8–14 phase (*The Learning Country*, WAG, 2001); and more recently the development of a national pedagogy strategy and school effectiveness framework.

Full implementation of *Curriculum for Excellence* in Scotland from August 2010 was preceded by a dedicated 'engagement year' (2009) for systematic trialling of draft Experiences and Outcomes and further consultation with the profession and a wide range of other stakeholders including local authorities, universities and colleges, parent groups and third sector organisations (University of Glasgow, 2009). This was the culmination of a consultative approach which began with the National Debate on Education in 2002. A Curriculum Review Group set up in 2003 was asked by the Scottish Ministers to take account of the views expressed in the National Debate, current research and international comparisons and global factors. The overall architecture was developed over a three-year period.

The above review restates the position that curriculum is an evolving process and that due attention needs to be afforded to the history and politics of curriculum making. Much can be learned from tracing the trajectories of policies. This includes attention to the composition (and size) of the policy community, shifting levels of influence among those policy actors (or 'policy entrepreneurs') who seek to shape the curriculum, and the extent and impact on policy of processes of consultation and engagement with the profession and wider community. With the need to consider the implications for continuing change in a fast moving globalised world the curriculum for the future will be under constant review to remain relevant to the needs of learners.

Key questions for reflection

Identify a recent curriculum change. To what extent was this change influenced by processes of consultation and engagement?

What are the international dimensions that have affected national curriculum development in your country?

How does the notion of travelling policy contribute to our understanding of curriculum policy in the UK?

Conclusion

The analysis of curriculum development from a comparative perspective has raised questions concerning the what, how and why of curriculum development. Chapter 2 discussed three key themes which emerged in primary schooling – 'basic skills', 'subjects' (and knowledge) and 'the child'. Despite the constantly changing contexts for education it appears that these three themes continue to feature in discussions of curriculum design in the UK, albeit with different degrees of emphasis in the four countries. Similarly, discussions considering the curriculum of the primary school in terms of activity and experience, rather than of knowledge to be acquired and facts to be stored, originating from views raised in the Hadow Report (1931) also continue to feature. The comparative analysis has shown that it is not possible to separate the primary curriculum from questions of approaches to teaching and learning ('pedagogy'), or from the ways in which children and their learning are assessed or the contexts in which they live and learn.

Curriculum development starts from questions that interrogate the purpose of education in the twenty-first century and consider how people learn best. The answers to purpose will determine what the curriculum looks like and how it is implemented. Chapter 3 pointed out that national curricula are built on particular conceptions of knowledge, and views about how people learn. Tensions will inevitably arise where differing views about the purpose of education are held. For example, how questions are answered about emphasis on literacy, numeracy, science, creativity or citizenship in curriculum design and implementation are at the heart of views about the purpose of education. Differences in opinion about these important questions highlight the importance of ongoing review and negotiation of the curriculum and its implementation. As suggested in Chapter 2:

> We should not see the primary curriculum as being fixed, but rather as the present manifestation of a continuously evolving debate about what it is that younger children should be learning, in terms of knowledge and concepts, skills and dispositions. This debate reflects changing priorities in society and changing views about the relationship between primary schooling and what precedes and succeeds it, that is provision for the early years and secondary school provision respectively.

An increase in decision making devolved to schools, which means that teachers and pupils have more freedom to determine what has to be learned, will make learning more relevant to local needs and is more likely to motivate and engage learners in their own learning. The example presented in Chapter 3 of Alec starting a lesson suggests that he believes his role as a teacher is to enable children to make choices in their learning. Furthermore that Alec believes that when children make choices they are often more motivated, and that higher motivation leads to better outcomes. The growing emphasis on co-constructing learning, self-determination and self-regulation, flexibility, adaptability and creativity does not sit well within a prescriptive centrally determined curriculum. Chapter 4 highlighted the tensions that teachers are experiencing in achieving a balance between the ideals of child-centred learning and the requirement to work to a national curriculum.

A prescriptive mandatory national curriculum leaves teachers feeling de-skilled, de-professionalised and frustrated on a daily basis when they feel unable to adapt the curriculum to the needs and motivations of their pupils. However, it is recognised that a curriculum framework is needed to guide teachers' work and pupils' learning. Chapter 3 sets out White's argument for an aims-informed curriculum, on the grounds that, in a democracy, because the curriculum has an impact on the shape of future society, its content should not be left wholly to the discretion of teachers. Rather teachers should be guided by a clearly articulated set of aims but should retain the freedom to decide how best to organise curriculum delivery at local level, taking into consideration pupils' interests and backgrounds, the character of the local community and school resources (White 2004). The overarching aims of the curriculum in the UK countries were presented in Chapter 3. It was noted that the most striking difference between the countries' approach is that taken by Wales. The broad aims for education are located within the framework of the United Nations Convention of the Rights of the Child (UNCRC). This is a powerful signal that children's rights are important and should be a central feature of any national curriculum.

Chapter 3 also makes the point that the apparent simplicity of an objectives-driven approach masks a number of tensions relating to the nature of objectives, for example, the potential of inappropriately emphasising some and neglecting others; the associated danger of emphasising trivial rather than significant aspects of learning; the potentially limiting effect of pre-specified intentions; the associated danger of de-skilling teachers; the difficulty of predicting outcomes; and the neglect of unanticipated but potentially important outcomes. The challenges of proposing a curriculum framework and addressing local, national and international policy making is what policy makers in the UK and beyond are wrestling with (Asia Society, 2011). What should the balance of control between local, national and international be in curriculum design and implementation?

The increasing shift towards schools having greater autonomy in decision making about the 'what and how of learning and teaching' has put greater pressure on the accountability of teachers and school leaders for the quality of pupil learning outcomes. This has resulted in more tightly controlled assessment systems in England for example. While, in Scotland, recent reviews of teaching and learning (Donaldson, 2011; McCormac, 2011) have proposed that there should be an increased emphasis on the professional commitment of teachers to self-evaluate their own practice, and take responsibility for continually improving their own knowledge and their teaching skills, in an effort to improve pupil learning.

Decisions about the aims, design and implementation of the curriculum for the future must be negotiated through dialogue, partnership and interactive processes that recognise teachers and pupils as curriculum developers and policy makers. Schools themselves should be recognised as sites of knowledge creation and should be encouraged to generate and evaluate diverse responses to the opportunities and challenges that arise through ongoing enquiry in learning and teaching. This does not imply that the curriculum is only about spontaneity, creativity and the freedom to follow the interest of the child. The primary school curriculum must provide children with a strong foundation to develop their own learning and support them in engaging with substantive concepts through enquiry, questioning and discussion. Curriculum, pedagogy and assessment must be developed together. As Chapter 5 suggested, curriculum defines what is to be learned and pedagogy describes how learning takes place with the role of assessment being to gather evidence to support learning and allow all to discern the extent to which learning is taking place. Teachers play a key role in creating stimulating learning environments that enable children to engage with different forms of knowledge in ways that make sense to them. This is likely to include some subject teaching but will also see different forms of knowledge being explored and skills and dispositions being developed through integrated days according to local contexts. To be successful the curriculum for the future needs teachers and pupils to be central to the decision-making process at national, local and classroom levels. This requires teachers to be well informed through professional development that challenges their thinking about learning and teaching and involves ongoing inquiry into practice with peers, mentors and external critical friends. It will also require the development of trust between those working at national, local and classroom levels, and recognition that they are all partners in policy making, implementation and assessment.

Teacher education/training task

Choose an area of curriculum policy presented in this volume and consider the extent to which it is evidence-based. How is evidence used to make a case for change? How robust is the evidence?

Identify who are the key people and organisations that contributed to the development of a curriculum policy and the associated pedagogy.

Consider the extent to which the influence of individuals and agencies within the policy community has changed over time.

Further reading

Law, E.H. and Nieveen, N. (eds) (2010) *Schools as Curriculum Agencies. Asian and European Perspectives on School-Based Curriculum Development.* Rotterdam: Sense Publishers.
This book offers an overview of the major trends and challenges of school-level curriculum development based on insights and experiences from 13 countries.
RSA (2011) *The RSA Area-Based Curriculum: Engaging the Local.* Available at: www.thersa.org/projects/education/area-based-curriculum.
This report outlines the case for a school curriculum that is co-created by teachers, young people, community members and local organisations.

References

Asia Society (2011) *Improving Teacher Quality Around the World.* Available at: http://asiasociety.org/files/lwtw-teachersummitreport0611.pdf.
Assessment Reform Group (2002) *Assessment for Learning: 10 Principles.* Cambridge: University of Cambridge School of Education.
Ball, S.J. (1998) Big policies/small world: an introduction to international perspectives in educational policy, *Comparative Education*, 34(2), 117–131.
Braun, A., Maguire, M. and Ball, S.J. (2010) Policy enactments in the UK secondary school: examining policy, practice and school positioning, *Journal of Education Policy*, 25(4), 547–560.
Centre for the Use of Research and Evidence in Education (CUREE) (2005) National Framework for Mentoring and Coaching. Available at: www.curee.co.uk/files/publication/1219925968/National-framework-for-mentoring-and-coaching.pdf.
Cochran-Smith, M. and Lytle, S.L. (eds) (2009) *Inquiry as Stance. Practitioner Research for the Next Generation.* New York: Teacher College Press.
Commission of the European Communities (2007) *Schools for the Twenty-First Century.* Available at: http://ec.europa.eu/education/school21/consultdoc_en.pdf.
Crossley, M. and Watson, K. (2003) *Comparative and International Research in Education: Globalisation, Context and Difference.* London: Routledge.
Department for Education (2010) *The Importance of Teaching. The Schools White Paper 2010.* London: The Stationery Office.
Donaldson, G. (2011) *Teaching Scotland's Future.* Edinburgh: The Scottish Government.
Hadow, W.H. (1931) *The Primary School.* Report of the Consultative Committee. London: HMSO.

Hoyle, E. (1974). Professionality, professionalism and control in teaching, *London Education Review*, 3(2), 13–19.

Jones, K. and Alexiadou, N. (2001) Travelling policy: local spaces. Paper in 'The Global and the National: Reflections on the Experience of Three European States' symposium at the European Conference on Educational Research (ECER), Lille, September.

Law, E.H. and Nieveen, N. (eds) (2010) *Schools as Curriculum Agencies. Asian and European Perspectives on School-Based Curriculum Development*. Rotterdam: Sense Publishers.

Lawton, D. (1989) *Education, Culture and the National Curriculum*. London: Hodder & Stoughton.

Levin, B. (1998) An epidemic of education policy: (what) can we learn from each other? *Comparative Education*, 34(2), 131–141.

Livingston, K. and Colucci-Gray, L. (2006) Scottish teachers for a new era: where should we start from, if not together? *Education in the North*, 14, 36–37.

McCormac, G. (2011) *Advancing Professionalism in Teaching: The Report of the Review of Teacher Employment in Scotland*. Available at: www.scotland.gov.uk/Resource/Doc/920/0120 759.PDF.

Menter, I., Hulme, M., Elliot, D., Lewin, J., Baumfield, V., Britton, A., Carroll, M., Livingston, K., McCulloch, M., McQueen, I., Patrick, F. and Townsend, A. (2010) *Literature Review on Teacher Education in the 21st Century*. Edinburgh: The Scottish Government.

Ontario (2008) *Reach Every Student: Energising Ontario Education*. Available at: www.edu.gov. on.ca/eng/document/energize/energize.pdf.

Organisation for Economic Cooperation and Development (OECD) (2009) *Creating Effective Teaching and Learning Environments. First Results from TALIS*. Available at: www.oecd.org/ dataoecd/17/51/43023606.pdf

Ozga, J. (2005) Models of policy making and policy learning. Discussion Paper for the Seminar on Policy Learning in 14–19 Education. Joint seminar of Education and Youth Transitions Project and Nuffield Review, 15 March 2005.

Ozga, J. and Jones, R. (2006) Travelling and embedded policy: the case of knowledge transfer, *Journal of Education Policy*, 21(1), 1–17.

Phillips, D. (2006) Investigating policy attraction in education, *Oxford Review of Education*, 32(5), 551–559.

Phillips, D. and Ochs, K. (2004) *Educational Policy Borrowing: Historical Perspectives*. Oxford: Symposium.

Sachs, J. (2003) *The Activist Teaching Profession*. Buckingham: Open University Press.

Salo, P., Furu, M. and Ronnerman, K. (2008) Educational policies and reforms: a Nordic perspective. In Ronnerman, K., Furu, E.M. and Salo, P. (eds) *Nurturing Praxis: Action Research in Partnerships between School and University in a Nordic Light*. Rotterdam: Sense Publishers (pp. 11–20).

Steiner-Khamsi, G. (ed.) (2004) *The Global Politics of Educational Borrowing and Lending*. New York: Teachers College Press.

Tatto, M.T. (2007) *Reforming Teaching Globally*. Didcot: Symposium.

Timperley, H., Wilson, A., Barrar, H. and Fung, I. (2007) *Teacher Professional Learning and Development: Best Evidence Synthesis Iteration (BES)*. Available at: www.educationcounts.govt. nz/__data/assets/pdf_file/0017/16901/TPLandDBESentire.pdf.

University of Glasgow (2009) Curriculum for Excellence Draft Experiences and Outcomes: Collection, Analysis and Reporting of Data: Final Report. Project Report. Learning and Teaching Scotland, Glasgow, UK.

Van Den Akker, J., Gravemeijer, K., McKenney, S. and Nieveen, N. (eds) (2006) *Educational Design Research*. London: Routledge.

Wallace, I. (1994) The Northern Ireland Curriculum – solving actual problems, *Curriculum Journal*, 5(1), 31–41.

Weis, L. and Fine, M. (2001) Extraordinary conversations in public schools. *Qualitative Studies in Education*, 14(4), 497–523.

Welsh Assembly Government (WAG) (2001) *The Learning Country: A Paving Document*. Cardiff: Welsh Assembly Government.

White, J. (ed.) (2004) *Rethinking the School Curriculum: Values, Aims and Purposes*. London: RoutledgeFalmer.

Wiliam, D. (2007) Content then process: teacher learning communities in the service of formative assessment. In Reeves, D. (ed.) *Ahead of the Curve: The Power of Assessment to Transform Teaching and Learning*. Bloomington, IN: Solution Tree (pp. 184–204).

Index